INSIDE OUT

Prison, Poetry & Perseverance

Michael L. Graham

11-4-16

RICHARD JACKSON
INSIDE OUT
Prison, Poetry & Perseverance
ISBN-13 978-1505870787
ISBN-10 150587078X

Published by
BALM2 Ministries
Bishop Archie L. McInnis, II
Brooklyn, NY

Edited by The BALM2 Editing Team
Wanza Leftwich
Cynthia McInnis

Cover design by Jason McIntosh
5dCreative.com

DEDICATION

To my big brother, Leonard A. Jackson for never turning his back on me, demonstrating that we have to move forward because failure is never an option and for loving me for me.
I love and appreciate you big brother.

IN MEMORY OF

Hiram Thomas Jackson, daddy I love and miss you so much.
Thanks for the blueprint.

Evelyn Mary Warner, who also challenged me to achieve more;

Mildred Byers, who put me straight;

Irvin (Butch) Atkins for talking to me like no other man;

Eddie (Kibaka) Ellis, the father of the Resurrection Study Group who saw qualities in me that I did not see in myself and strategically brought them out.

Sherieff Clayton, my beloved brother and comrade who is missed every day of my life. His legacy is inbred in RESURRECTION!

ACKNOWLEDGEMENTS

To my wife Keisha for loving me and holding down,

My son Keyshon for being all a son could be. I am so proud of you,

To Bishop Archie McInnis, II for demonstrating true friendship and spiritual guidance,

My grandmother Elizabeth Callender for always challenging me to do better,

To my mother Sharon Callender for always challenging me to do better,

To Edna Jackson for never giving up on me,

To Sandra Surita for her spiritual guidance and support,

To all my Resurrection Study Group Brothers,

To Walter Simpkins of Community Fathers Inc. for everything,

To Jamel Muhammad for demonstrating true Brotherhood and integrity,

To my big brother Plummer Bradley thank you for everything

Thanks to Mr. Garfield Zeitler and Dominic A. Dagostino for believing in me,

To all my peoples in Marcy Projects,

To the Kelsey Clan thanks for everything,

To Monifa thank you so much,

I did not forget my nephew Leonard A. Jackson Jr. you make me so proud. Thank you.

To Dupree (Turf)Harris, May you be home soon we all miss you. When Is enough, *enough*? Free Dupree Harris.

The Schenectady City Mission for all their support and the awesome staff.

Special thanks to Cynthia McInnis and Wanza Leftwich for editing my first book,

TABLE OF CONTENTS

A Letter to the Victim

Dear Mr. Foreman:

This has to be the hardest letter I have ever written. I do not know what I am going to say or how I am going to say it. All I know is that it is time I say something directly to you.

Mr. Foreman, it has been over two decades since I took your life. To be completely honest with you after the initial sleepless nights of tossing and turning, it was quite a while before your life or anyone else's life meant anything to me. I now know there can never be a legit reason for snatching God's most precious gift "LIFE" from another human being. God created us all and He is the only one that has the right to call us home. I would truly understand if you just stop reading this letter, tear it up or burn it because the fact remains and will always remain that the author of this letter murdered you in cold blood; the author denied you the opportunity to be a loving and supportive father to your five children; and the author snatched the heart right out of your wife and emotionally and mentally killed your mother. I can only imagine the hate, dislike and frustration you have for this author; me. However, I do humbly request that you read on. Not for me because I am nobody, a murderer, an inmate in a correctional facility serving a life sentence for taking your life. I ask that you read on for you because over the many years, I have asked myself hundreds of times why? I know you have asked yourself the same question multiple times.

This letter may not even answer that underlining question of why? But I do plan to give you a little clarity on the mindset of that heartless seventeen year old that caused your death on that cold January night. Mr. Foreman there is no justification that I can write to adequately explain or express why I took your life. I have been in prison now for twenty-four years. Over the years I have educated myself to a large degree. So I have the ability to utilize a lot of big words, throw some catchy phrases together and give you an explanation that would sound real good. But then what purpose would that serve in my overall attainment of atonement and for sure this would not be the hardest letter I have ever written. I am trying to be as real as I can be and find the words to express myself clearly, so please excuse me if I jump around at times in this letter.

Mr. Foreman I did not appreciate life at all. My interpretation of life was warped and consisted of getting so called paid and peer respect. Obtaining these two things are all I cared about because those were the two things in life that made me feel good. I know you're saying that is crazy but that was my reality as crazy as it sounds. I want to explain to you about the emotional and psychological abuse and turmoil that I was going through in my home; Also, my inability to communicate rationally with adults and peers without becoming violent or verbally abusive. But as you know millions of children and teens experience domestic violence in their homes grow up in poverty and dysfunctional communities and never commit a crime or take another man's life. The reason for that is because Mr. Foreman when it all comes to a head it comes down to personal decision-making. Every man makes his choices in life. That is what distinguishes animals from human beings. Humans have the ability to incorporate rational reasoning and not be driven by impulses. I chose to live the life I lived and I chose to be out that night, and I chose to pull that trigger thinking it would make me bigger. Now that is crazy to say the least, but understand in its truth I share a shame that is unexplainable.

I am not that seventeen year old anymore Mr. Foreman. I am trying my best not to say I am sorry because sorry is not enough for taking a man's life. Sorry was not violent; sorry was not running the streets and sorry did not have total disregard for human life. I am the sorry one for allowing my inability to communicate to propel me to take your precious life. I am the sorry one who allowed your children to grow up without a father; I am the sorry one who denied your sister a brother and grandchildren a grandfather. The words "I am sorry" can never be enough for you and for me as well. Mr. Foreman as you sit on your throne in Heaven with your beautiful wings spread wide looking down at this world that I took from you. I humbly ask can you please give me a muster of forgiveness. I know what I am asking for is a very large order but please understand or at least try to that over the years I have come to recognize the error of my ways and all of the collateral damage I have caused in so many innocent people's lives. It has been hard for me to forgive myself. I have replayed that night in my mind hundreds of times and the one question that always arises is, "Richard, why did you pull that trigger?" You more than anybody in this world know that I did not have to pull that trigger. Yes, you struggled as any would struggle finding him self accosted by thugs with a gun in a dark parking lot 3 O'clock in the morning. Can I blame it on you for being a man? Absolutely not! I must take full and total responsibility because it took a conscious thought to pull that trigger. As I have learned, "thought" is the father of "action." What was my thought process? My thought process at the time was: "How dare you struggle?" "Don't you know who I am?", "If you pull a gun you better use it.", "You know how the game: kill or be killed", "I cannot allow you to revenge this robbery."

My thought process was twisted, shaped and molded by the streets. That is what made it easy for me to pull the trigger. Did I know right from wrong? Yes! I knew what I was doing was wrong but it felt right and my adherence to the street code had me believing it was right.

Mr. Foreman, I know this makes no sense to you and most likely you cannot believe that I have the nerve to express to you these attitudes and behaviors. Well, it took me twenty-four years to work up the nerve. I need to tell you in plain English and humbly ask your forgiveness. Over the years, I have searched my soul, sought information, beat myself up and reached out to a psychologist. All in a sincere effort to figure out how does a seventeen year old put a shotgun to the back of a man's head and pull the trigger? I needed to know that answer. I have shared my mindset with you but the deep-rooted issue is what now has society's youth running aimlessly and violently. It is as simple as "LOVE." I did not love myself and that made it easier to hate others, made it easy to inflict pain on others and ultimately take your life Mr. Foreman. You were not a total stranger to me, Mr. Foreman. I saw you around the projects for years and most likely you witnessed me grow up. However, I did not have an ounce of compassion for you or that ounce could have saved both of our lives. For compassion to exist there must be love. I should have been able to look at you and see my father, my brother or my uncle. But no! Street life and a lack of love for myself and for everything around me, had veils over my eyes.

Once again I can never justify taking your precious life and denying you the opportunity of being a father. I am just attempting to come clean with you and let you know I was not in my God given state of mind. Nevertheless, I have a brother who is a couple of months older than me and he experienced all of the hardships, psychological abuse, neglect and so forth as I did growing up in Marcy Projects. But you know what Mr. Foreman he has never committed one crime. That is because he consciously made good choices and saw our social-economic conditions and life's adversities as obstacles he had to overcome in order to be successful in life. I had those same obstacles and adversities as roadblocks to bust through. So ultimately, it becomes our responses to social stimuli that fashions our success or demise in life. Mr.

Foreman, I don't know that nothing I say can make you embrace me as your son or brother. Taking your life is something I live with and struggle with every day and I need for you to know that. I have utilized these years wisely by adequately addressing my thought process. I have completed many therapeutic classes, self-help groups, participated and facilitated leadership development classes. I have even been part of creating programs so that I can assist in helping other youth with their moral and mental development; I have even acquired a college degree. You know what Mr. Foreman all that I have accomplished was because of your blood being spilt on that parking lot concrete ground but I have built on your death. It is bittersweet; bitter because I had to take another man's life and receive a life sentence in prison to recognize and address the errors of my ways. Sweet, because I can finally say that I am a changed man with conviction. I know for an actual fact that when I do walk out of this prison I am going to change hundreds if not thousands of youth's lives. I know I could never pay you back or society for taking your life but I will spend the rest of my life paying that debt by demonstrating to all that a man with the will and determination can change his life around in the New York State Department of Corrections. However, this change can only come when one truly recognizes his faults and the destruction that he or she has played part in destroying their very own community. Then he or she must atone for his action and commit him or herself to the resurrection of their mind and play a part in rebuilding what they once tore down.

Mr. Foreman, I hope that these words that I struggled with at times give you a little understanding of that seventeen year old on that cold January night some two and a half decades ago. Also, I warmly pray it sheds light on the forty-one year old I have evolved into today. These words come directly from my heart to offer you a sincere apology for my reckless behavior in taking your life. I have grown tremendously and will never again be a part of that lifestyle or mindset. Today, I have set the bar extremely high for myself and even though I may never reach it because of its height. I will strive for the rest of my life trying to reach it. I have a debt to pay and it is not just to society for taking your precious life away. It is a debt to you and your family, a debt that will forever be owed as long as I breathe. A debt that I am honored to pay because it is a part of my responsibility to you, to myself and to the larger society. And more than anything else, it is an intricate part of my sincere apology to you. I truly know that sorry is in no way enough but this letter would not be right if I didn't say with compassion "Yo, man, I am sorry.

Please find it in your heart to forgive me. I love you and myself today. Mr. Foreman, take care and if I don't hear from you I know you will be watching...

Sincerely,
Richard Jackson

CHAPTER ONE

Introduction to Personal Testimony

The Resurrection Study Group (RSG) is a youth leadership and personal development program created at the Green Haven Prison in Stormville, New York, in September 1989 by Eddie Ellis. The focal points of the program are the development of youth leaders, peer role models and problem-solvers through the creation of the "New African Man". The program model uses non-traditional approaches to criminal and social justice issues that emphasize community empowerment.

In September 1989, I did not seek out the Resurrection Study Group. They chose me to be a member mainly because I was one of the youngest prisoners in the prison at that time. I did not even want to attend the first class. An older brother that was in the class just happened to lock on my housing unit and he literally dragged me to the first class kicking, scratching and cursing. When I got to the class, of course, I was the youngest one there. I chose a seat in the far back of the room.

Eddie Ellis started the class and my first impression of him was, "Who is this Old Cat? He can't tell me jack. I'm out of here on the early go back!"

I don't remember how he started the class. It's all a blur because ninety percent of his spill was way over my head. He spoke on topics like Pan-Africanism, Afro-centricity, Community Empowerment and Political Control that were just not in my world. What was eerie about that first class is that it seemed as though he kept his eyes on me; and every word he said was directly for me. It was like the other twenty-nine men were not in the room.

What first caught my attention was that this Old Cat had been doing time since the early seventies. Secondly, he started talking about popular culture and how the youth of that day was losing touch with their inherited values and getting caught up in a manufactured value system.

Lastly, he talked about the importance for prisoners to maintain and strengthen their family values. That was something that I was definitely lacking at that time in my life. At that moment something in me clicked and I opted not to go back on the early go back; not that they would have let me. This was surely one of the best decisions of my life.

I attended the class the next week and the week after. The Resurrection Study Group was starting to have a major impact on my life. The group realized early on that we were doing some very serious work and that we needed more class time. Soon thereafter, we met three times a week. I attended every class and I did not need anyone to drag me down there. In fact, I made sure other brothers were going. I was now absorbing concepts and ideologies that were over my head in the first class. The Resurrection brothers had extreme patience with me.

There were times when I tried to grasp a particular concept and every brother would get up and give me his understanding of that concept until I got it right. They never talked down to me or shunned me for my lack of knowledge. They showered me with Big Brother love and constantly instilled in me that I was the future of Resurrection; the future of the youth and our future leader. These were some very heavy responsibilities. However, my Resurrection brothers gave me the motivation to live up to them.

The Resurrection Study Group had a "Cadre Leadership" ideology. We traced our history, pinpointed our effective major leaders and viewed their assassinations. The Resurrection Study Group vowed not to create just one leader but a cadre of leaders for the people. As a result, no one could ever eliminate the Resurrection Study Group and its leaders and its teaching could live on forever. Our ideology will forever live on and touch the minds and souls of our youth. Our cadre leadership ideology was soon tried and tested.

In 1991, the Green Haven Correctional Facility transferred Eddie Ellis to the Woodbourne Correctional Facility. This crushed the group emotionally, but we moved on. Over two decades later, the Resurrection

Study Group is still alive and resurrecting youth leadership inside of the New York State Department of Corrections and in the community at large.

In 1990, during a Black History month celebration, they gave me the opportunity to give my personal testimony about being a part of the RSG. The following is the speech that I delivered. I was scared to death, but I delivered it. The Green Haven Correctional Facility's general population received the speech very well. The RSG has changed the lives of hundreds of young Black men within the New York State Prison system. I am just one example of many. What is unique about the RSG is that it contends that prisons must no longer be used as "warehouses" for social control which continues to produce high recidivism rates; instead, they must be transformed into universities of higher education that empowers an individual to maintain a productive life upon release.

The Resurrection Study Group cites the Malcolm X model as a ripe fruit plucked, Nelson Mandela as an overripe fruit finally plucked, and George Jackson as a ripe fruit not plucked. The process of resurrection must be the measurement for determining ripe fruits and the community should have the power to pluck.

CHAPTER TWO
Personal Testimony

Due to my incarceration my name is Richard R. Jackson, 86B2070. However, due to my level of consciousness my name is Ausar, Black god. I am a member of the Resurrection Study Group. I would like to share my personal testimony and general benefits of being in the Resurrection Study Group. It has taught me a great deal about life. When I first entered the Resurrection Study Group, I had no sense of true life. I was just living day by day.

When I was seventeen years old, I was incarcerated. I am now twenty-one years old and fully resurrected to the New African Man; a man with an obligation to be a positive role model for the youth. I owe it all to Resurrection. When I first came into to the Resurrection Study Group it was around Kwanzaa time. This was the first time in my life I really received a sense of family. Like many youth, I came from a household headed by a woman and did not really know the true meaning of the extended family. So, my childhood was somewhat missing that family unit. I always had a good idea of what family was but it was not until I entered Resurrection and participated in the celebration of Kwanzaa that I truly received what a family was and its proper functions.

During our seven day celebration I was around brothers that were willing to help, willing to share, willing to teach and most importantly, brothers that cared. They really gave me a sense of belonging. When I entered the room I felt the electricity that these brothers generated. I love every one of those brothers for showing me what family is all about.

Many people take their family for granted and do not really know the true value of having a family. As for me, I am just getting my family and values together thanks to the Resurrection Study Group. You see before I entered Resurrection the only contact that I had with my family was with my brother. I felt that I did not need a family that I could do this time by myself. Due to this frame of mind, I disregarded all family contact with my mother, father, uncles, aunts, etc. A family did not mean anything to me.

While incarcerated, my mother took the blame. She felt that she went wrong somewhere in raising me. She felt she was not a proper mother and she could not bear the fact that her baby boy was in prison at 17 years old and not eligible to return home until 35 years of age. This was just too much for her and she underwent several severe emotional breakdowns and saw her death bed twice. After those ordeals, I still did not know the true meaning of family nor did I try to reach out to my mother or any other part of my family. In fact, it made me rebel from my mother even more because I always saw her as being strong; the head of the house, the one that took the good with the bad. Then, I saw her as being weak. My rebellion of my mother got so bad that I remember discussing her one time with a brother in Resurrection and referring to her as a B****. This statement shocked the brother so bad that he was speechless for a good while. When he did regain his composure, I had a lesson that changed my life and gave me a whole different meaning of Resurrection and family.

In the Resurrection Study Group, I learned that the plight of the single Black mother is a hard and enduring one. She takes great pride in her offspring because they are a part of her soul, her present sufferings and future struggles. Also, her blood and sweat is not in vain because she is working hard to make a better life for her offspring. I came to realize what my mother was going through and most importantly my lack of not having a strong sense of family.

The Resurrection Study Group also taught me that I was not alone in my analysis of the Black Family. Many people and especially the black youth have to go through ordeals such as mine to know and understand the true meaning of family. This is why Resurrection is such a good study group; it can show you and teach you the true meaning of family before you go through ordeals like mine. If every youth in prison and in the free world can get into programs like Resurrection and taught the need of a family unit, the Black race will be in a much better state. The youth of today will grow up loving one another and not killing each other. The only reason the youth of today are killing one another is because they do not know what brotherly love is. And they do not have a sense of family. If they had a sense of love, they will know who their real enemies are. Resurrection places great emphasis on family because Resurrection sees the need to resurrect the black family on these things.

Let us take a brief look at our African history. Our ancestors practiced that every adult female was mother and every adult male was a father. So all the children of the village did not just have one mother or one father because everyone was family and everyone was in harmony with each other. Most importantly, everyone respected each other. These are the values we, as African men must pick back up and start to institute them not only in our homes but in our communities as well. We are one race with one aim and one goal. Let us be one family and resurrect each other to our true and original family values.

Frances Cress Welsing had a very strong sense of family in mind and the need to implement this to the black youth. She said, "Whether or not we yet recognize it, Black children are our most valuable possession and our very greatest resource potential. Any meaningful discussion as to the survival or the future of the Black family as whole depends upon the maximal development of all Black children. Children are the only future of any people; if the children's lives are squandered and if the children of a people are not fully developed at whatever cost or sacrifice and by all necessary means, then the people themselves will have co-signed themselves to a certain death. They will be destroyed either from within or from without by the attack of their own children against them." Frances Cress Welsing, is a very strong Black woman with the knowledge and understanding of the need to resurrect the Black family.

We, as a people, are in a very deadly situation and are in a race against time. We must start looking at our problems with a critical eye and the foundation of our problem is that we have lost touch with our original family values; The Black man more so than the Black woman. I do not mean to step on any toes and I know that there are crime generative factors that also account for this but we still have to get our families back together. Statistics shows that over seventy percent of our urban homes are run by the Black woman. Black men, let me share a little history with you. During the North Atlantic Slave Trade, the oppressor did not have too much of a problem bringing the Black woman into slavery. Once the oppressor captured the man of the family, the Black woman was so dedicated that at the time she went along willingly to stand by the side of her Black man. Is this how we repay that dedication from the Black women by deserting them and having them lead over 70% of the urban homes? I think it is about time we as Black men stop being European value followers and start being African value fathers. This is the only way we can bring our race back to its proper place; to being Kings and Queens and living as one.

The Resurrection Study Group is teaching all men to be fathers; not just any kind of fathers but responsible, loving, hardworking and most importantly Pan-African fathers. All members could not have gotten to this level of understanding and knowledge of what a strong sense of family consisted of or how to be a true father if a Pan-African father would not have stepped up and taught us the meaning of resurrection and a sense of family.

So, in conclusion, and on behalf of the whole Resurrection Study Group, we would like to give true thanks to the father of Resurrection and the father of all our hearts, Eddie Ellis (Kababka).

CHAPTER THREE
Perception of Time

Time revolves around circumstances and situations. Our perception of time is defined by how we live it. The social stimulus it encounters and our rational thinking in navigating us through it. This is something that took me many, many years to conceptualize and incorporate into my daily living and mindset.

It has really taken me a considerable amount of time and hardships that almost mentally and physically crippled me to truly appreciate time. It is kind of ironic because I am doing time, a life time as some may term it. The Honorable Judge Joseph Larmbado's term of incarceration for me in September of 1986 was seventeen and a half years to life. At that time in my life, I did not retain the capacity to truly understand what the sentence in terms of time really meant. I was seventeen and half years old at the time of sentencing. All I had the mental capacity to do was to calculate seventeen and a half and seventeen a half years equaled thirty-five. So in my feeble mind, I consumed the thought and idea that I would be freed from my physical incarceration at thirty-five years of age. All I had to do was the TIME! I had not a clue of the mental incarceration that held me captive.

My perception of time started to take shape on October 16, 1986 when I was transferred from Rikers Island to Elmira Correctional Facility. I was transported on a Greyhound-style bus with about forty other adolescents. Two Police Officers stood in the front of the bus with loaded revolvers itching for a reason to pull the trigger and two Police Officers in the back of the bus. One had a revolver and the same itchy finger and one with a double barrel shotgun. Once we boarded onto the buses, they read us the riot act; which was very convincing and chilling at the same time. The bus ride from Rikers Island to Elmira Correctional Facility took approximately eight hours counting the pit stops and scenic routes. The longest bus ride I had ever taken. As I looked out the window, in a daze, during the ride to Elmira Correctional Facility, I witnessed the brick building, concrete sidewalks and traffic lights turn into houses, green pastures then tall mountains. I began to realize then that my terrain was dramatically changing. I was literally headed into a time warp where time would pass by but my surrounding environment would not change.

As the bus neared Elmira Correctional Facility, shackled, scared and not knowing what would unfold in time, I saw the biggest, ugliest gray and dirty concrete wall. This egregious wall surrounded Elmira Correctional Facility and seemed as though it took on a life of itself. The steel gate suddenly opened and granted our bus passage inside Elmira Correctional Facility. Once inside the wall the bus stopped in front of a large granite or steel statue of a much older man hugging a pre-teen. All sorts of thoughts went through my head for the meaning of this statue. I know when I stepped off that bus, shackled; hand waist and legs, I said, "Richard, you are with the big boys now and that is what time it is." The egregious, concrete gray wall and the ambivalent meaning of the statue had me scared to death of both my security and the unexpected.

All forty of us adolescents were then marched inside the receiving room of Elmira Correctional Facility and ordered to strip down to our undergarments. There were a lot of whispers and screwed up faces but everyone followed the order and stripped down. In that spacious receiving room there were two barber chairs in the far right corner and one was where our hair was cut off. After our hair was cut, one by one, we were given a disposable razor and ordered to shave the hair off of our faces. I can remember turning to the officer and telling him I did not have any hair on my face. As 99% of us adolescents did not have a spec of facial hair. Why did I have to be the one to open my big mouth? That officer put his face so close to mine I could smell the coffee and tobacco on his breath. He screamed in my face releasing spittle all over my face. "Didn't I say cut all your facial hair off city boy? Now stop running your d*** mouth and cut that f***ing peach fuzz off of your face."

I wanted to respond but I instinctively knew I could not win this one. So I cut the peach fuzz off my face, all the while steaming on the inside. After the hair episode, we were made to strip naked and line up facing a wall. An officer with what looked like a fire extinguisher proceeded down the line of prisoners spraying us with a pesticide under our armpits on our private parts and around our anus area. After we were fumigated and made to stand naked in place for about fifteen minutes, a time span that seemed like an eternity, we were then marched into the shower and made to wash with a yellow soap that had dye in it. After the shower, I could feel my skin drying up and cracking. This ordeal at Elmira Correctional Facility reception was by far the most humiliating process I had ever been through. At that time in my life was when I felt helpless, powerless and worthless.

Time went by slowly for the next two days. I received my state issued greens which consisted of four pairs of state green pants, three state green shirts, one white state shirt, three pairs of white socks, three underwear briefs and three t-shirts. Oh yeah! One pair of black fake leather state boots that made your feet colder in the winter and hotter in the summer and one pair of Chuck Taylor sneakers which made you feel like you were walking around barefoot. No more Fila's, Wallabees, Calvin Klein, etc. All the attire I and my peers were used to wearing was gone without a thought. That state issued clothing would be my attire for decades to come. I no longer retained the right to wake up in the morning and choose what I wanted to wear. The New York State Department of Corrections now not only told me what to wear but they also retained the right to tell me how to wear my attire, when to wear my attire and when I could send my attire to the laundry to be cleaned. I could remember sitting on my bunk and looking over at the plastic bag that held my state issued clothing. Inside was an 8x10 piece of paper with 86B2070 on it. This was my New York State identification number. I said to myself, I am not going to remember that long a** number. I look back at that thought today in my advanced mindset and laugh to myself. Not only did I memorize it backward and forward, I also must have written and spoken it a billion times over the years. This number 86B2070 had become my name. I was no longer Richard R. Jackson. I had become 86B2070 which means "86" is the year I was committed to the New York State Department of Corrections; "B" means I was a boy; adolescent when I was committed and "2070" means

I was the 2,070th adolescent to enter the New York State Department of Corrections in 1986. Not only did I lose the right to wear what I wanted wear, I also lost the basic right as a man to be addressed by my birth name. I had been reduced to a seven digit number in just a small matter of time.

The most significant emotional event that forced me to get a hold on my perception of time while at Elmira Correctional Facility reception center was the day I was scheduled to see my Department of Corrections Counselor. I do not even remember her name. All I can remember about the interview is her asking me a whole bunch of questions in regards to my family. She asked questions such as, "How old is your mother and father?" How many brothers and sisters do you have? Where and who did you live with prior to your incarceration?

The entire interview did not take more than ten minutes. Upon leaving her office, she gave me a piece of paper and said, "Mr. Jackson, these are your commitment papers. They outline how much time you must serve in the Department of Corrections."

I looked at her like yeah, yeah, yeah and I know how much time I have to serve; seventeen and a half years to life. What do you think I am a fool because I am young and Black? I folded the paper up and put it in my back pocket. Now, that I look back on it, the rest of the day was a blur. However, I do remember that night going to the yard and meeting up with some friends. It was one of those bitterly cold October nights. The type of cold that is so bitter that once it gets into your bones you do not feel it anymore, you just become numb. I and my friends just stood out there talking about who was able to sneak their razor in and what prisons we wanted to be transferred to. As tough as we thought we were, none of us had the guts to really talk about the fears we were holding inside. Not one of us mentioned that ugly wall or that statue that had a lasting impression on all of us. I guess it was those fears that kept us warm in that bitter cold. When the yard closed we all picked our heads up, threw on our masks and gave each other pounds and headed back to our cells to lock in. Hours later, as I was prepared to go to bed, I took off my state green pants and the commitment papers that the counselor gave me earlier that day fell out of my back pocket. I picked it up, sat down on the end of my bunk, got some light from the hallway night light and began to read. This was the first time that I even looked at the commitment papers. What directly backhanded me in my face were two lines: my Conditional Release Date and my Maximum Release Date.

Conditional Release Date: 999 999 999 999
Maximum Release Date: 999 999 999 999

The total reality of my situation really hit me. It was like a Mack truck hitting a steel wall at optimal speed. I sat there on the end of my bunk with briefs and a T-shirt on and just started crying. Not a hysterical cry. But the cry you cry when a love one dies suddenly, the cry you cry when the pain inside has no-where to go so it comes out. "999 999 999 999" at that tender age was just inconceivable for me. My whole young life started to play itself before me; Time period after time period, poor decision after poor decision. I, for the first time started to evaluate my life for what it turned out to be and beat myself up mentally while the tears trickled down my face on to my lap. I began to realize that I did not have to do the things I did to get me into prison for a life sentence. Time kept punching me in the face and made the tears come down even harder. I tried to mentally put my tough guy act on and stop crying but I was powerless to do so. Those tears were the beginning of my soul being cleansed but I did not understand it. I just sat there paralyzed, crying and crying. Knowing I would spend decades in prison, decades on defense, decades away from my family, decades blocking knife thrusts and razor swings, decades regretting my poor decision making. I was afraid that I would not be able to do the time and that made the tears come down even harder. Something deep in me told me, "Richard, you are going to do this time and you are going to change your life." But I honestly at the time did not know how. I had never cried like I did on October 19, 1986. After that day, I can now look back and say, I went into a state of functional depression. I began to lash out at others for small things, mainly picking fights because I wanted others to feel my pain. I was consciously getting myself into trouble so I could be confined to my cell for 23 hours a day. I also began to limit my contact with my family and loved ones and began sleeping all day. I was slipping into a deep medicated state without the medication. Feeling sorry for myself became my mode of thought and the sorrier I felt for myself the sorrier I became in my everyday actions. I just could not erase the "999 999 999 999" from my mind. In essence, I was thinking and believing that my life was over. Like in the movie, "Green Mile" I was a "Dead Man Walking." That best describes my state of mind.

I walked around in this comatose state of mind for almost a year; Living very destructively because I allowed "999 999 999 999" to add tremendously to my warped perception of time. I also allowed "999 999 999 999" to be the justification for my continuous violent behavior. This comatose state of mind went on until I received my first visit upstate New York at Coxsackie Correctional Facility from my older brother. My older brother is only a little over seven months older than me. My older brother and I grew up as twins and were inseparable. We are so much alike that he can start a thought and I can finish it without skipping a beat. My brother and I have a saying that embodies our unbreakable bond, "We are all we got". When I walked into that visiting room and saw and hugged my big brother it gave me an unexplainable energy. When he looked at me it was as though he was looking right through me. I could never fool my Big Bro. He spoke some very simple words that resurrected my spirit and gave me a brand new lease on life.

He said "Richard, you have a family and we love you." My eyes welled up with tears and all I could do was hug my brother. Because those words alone let me know in the most clearest way that "999 999 999 999" was something that I did not have to bear on my shoulders all alone; that my family was there to help me with the heavy burden of "999 999 999 999" regardless of my bad choices and down-right stupidity. With the help of my family, I began to conceptualize that I could tackle this "999 999 999 999". Even though both my and my brother's lives had taken on opposing paths,, our love, loyalty and alliance to one another has stayed on course throughout the years. My perception about time as well as life dramatically changed that day on the visit my big brother. I realized that it was on me to navigate myself through the time I had to do; That no one or nothing had the power to do it but me, not even the mental influence ability of "999 999 999 999". I had to start thinking rationally and not allow the negative stimulus in my environment to dictate my actions. Most importantly, that situations and circumstances are not etched in stone or able to dictate the outcome of our future. Time is infinite and if I do not take one day at a time it can cripple me and define me. 'Forever forward and not one step backward!!!" I now understand what "TIME" is and its WORTH. But more then that I have come to love and appreciate time as well as life. So take the time out to read this once again.

CHAPTER FOUR
The Walk Down Life's Path

When we walk the path of life our only instructions are our experiences. Many of us walk the path of life stopping at all intersections asking whomever for directions hoping that they can make our walk easier. However, we sometimes realize too late in our walk down the path of life that the people we are requesting directions from are walking the same walk we are walking.

The path of life could be a long walk or a short walk. It all depends on how we walk. It depends upon what we learn while walking and most importantly, utilizing the things we learn to make our walk easier. There will be many corner stores, pot holes, stick-up men, drug dealers, CEO pimps, unlimited opportunities and a slew of distractions, attractions and illusion satisfactions. It is on the one walking to weigh his or her options so that they may continue to walk and not be hindered or blind-sided during their walk down the path of life.

Many people have remained on specific blocks or intersections on their walk down life's path because they have found comfort and familiarity. The fear of the unknown paralyzes them. They halt their walk and become a fixture in a place where they feel safe. However, life goes on and those who remain a glued fixture to a specific block or intersection watch others who are pursuing their walk down life's path walk right by.

It is easy to develop habits, kinks, self-isolation and a criminal mind along the path of life because this walk is not an easy walk and some of those walking this tedious walk look for a comfort outside of themselves. Life's path has no major rules or laws. Its only request is that you breathe. Breathing becomes easy but the walk down life's path gets harder mainly because those walking pick up things that they want instead of things that they need. They say experience is the best teacher but life's path has a way of making us forget our previous mishaps. So we hold on to those comforts outside of ourselves because they are easier to remember and can be found on every block or intersection.

Everyone's life path is guided by a special light; a light to guide us along the path in darkness. A light that allows us to use rational thought over guess work. A light that talks to our sub-conscious and reason with our conscious thought. It is a light that brings in to view the next block or intersection on our path down life's road. It gives direction to our imperfections. It is light that gives us courage to fight and insight to do right but it is on those walking down the path of life to recognize the light and not let the brightness of the light blind them.

One will meet, encounter and also interact with many characters, individuals and funny style people on life's path. Friends are a wonderful thing to have while on the journey down life's path. However, friends can be impediments to one's continued movement down life's path. Happiness breeds envy and envy breeds contempt. As a result, picking one's friends on the journey down life's path is a difficult task that one must ensue with caution and objectiveness. One must not be afraid to travel alone with one's thoughts and ideas. A friend can help in the tedious journey down life's path; but our best and most trusted friend is our self.

The journey down life's path is a beautiful experience that will teach us great lessons with every step. However, the lessons mean nothing if they are not internalized and acted upon with each movement along life's path. We will display many emotions including anger, frustration, despair, and hopelessness to name a few. These types of emotions can consume one to the extent that one gets stuck in a paralysis of analysis. One tries to figure out the root cause of emotional turmoil that impedes our development and do not learn until later on in life that we must keep it moving. Emotions are a part of life. How we deal with them must be based on our own life's lessons learned not that of others. We are each very unique people and what works for another might not necessarily work for us. Never forget a lesson learned for that same emotion is bound to rise again down life's path.

Nobody said life's path was going to be an easy walk. Nobody gives us a blueprint to navigate one's way down life's path. As one walks down life's path one cannot hold resentments for our actions or other people's actions that directly affect us. Resentment fosters hate because it sits on the heart and makes it cold all at the same time; draining our spirituality and keeping us away from inner peace that gives one the strength to journey down life's path with an open mind and vision to see life for what it is and not for what we want it to be. Resentment is a cancer that not only kills one from within it also infects the relationships with all those around us and kills them as well. There will be falls in life, there will be others whose sole purpose is to bring us down and there will be those that we just want to see buried. However, that path of life has no path called "get back lane" or an intersection named "cold heart expressway". The only direction is our previous experiences and the only guide is the light. Experiences can harbor resentments that can direct us down dead end roads or they can be utilized as lesson learned and give us an inner navigator system to follow the light of truth and peace.

Much can be elaborated about the path of life and its many pitfalls and unlimited opportunities. Therefore, what it essentially boils down to is individual choices. Yes, the environment factors in as well as society's norms and laws but one is still faced with his or her individual choices. Choices cannot be made out of emotional impulses that appease the ego and nothing else. Choices made on one's journey down the path of life must be made based on knowledgeable, rational decision making that can assist in one's continuous movement down life's path. There are no do overs in life; there is no built in eraser or whiteout. There is just that long or short journey before us and one's choices will ultimately determine how long or short one's walk down life's path is!

CHAPTER FIVE
The Inside Scoop for the Females

To my troopers, all those women who have stuck by their men while they were on lockdown, I salute you and praise you because I know the pain you endured, the shame you embraced and the loneliness you accepted and the happiness you denied and delayed so that you could stand by your man. I personally do not think there is a stronger woman out there. The proceeding words are not for you because you did and are doing what is necessary to build and maintain a solid relationship.

The brothers are going to be mad at me, rather, the lames are going to be mad at me for exposing their petty games. I am just tired of prisoners mistreating, misleading and not appreciating these women that go beyond the call of duty in supporting and standing by their man while he is incarcerated.

Ladies, I know and understand that the pool of good men in society is not the greatest. However, before you choose a man in prison do a little homework first. We are in the technological era. So it is nothing for you to go to the NYSDOC.GOV website, punch in your perspective friend's name and identification number. This way you can get a glimpse of what you are going to be working with. From this web site you can find out how much time he is serving, his earliest release date and what he is in prison for. Not that these things define a man, his worth or his potential in life; it just gives you a heads up and something to work with at your initial stage of dealing with this individual. It also saves you from jumping into a relationship head first with blinders on.

The first letter that a prisoner writes is very important and should be read very carefully. This is the image letter. The image he wants to project. Sometimes this is indeed the true image of the prisoner. Sometimes it is the image that the prisoner is projecting to gain a female's interest. It is on the female to see that all proceeding letters follow suit. When you talk with him over the phone see if he stays on line with what he has stated in his letters or if he even remembers what he wrote you. If you visit him, see if he can repeat what he said in his letters while looking you in your eyes. A lot of prisoners have developed their writing skills and they know exactly what a woman wants to hear. They can be very crafty in their letter writing. They are also prisoners that get other prisoners to write their letters for them. Any contradiction or back peddling in his letters should be addressed immediately. If the last paragraph of every letter is asking for something then it is time to give that brother the boot.

Many prisoners are very lonely and they do not have any one in their corner so they search out for pen pals, someone that they can write and build a friendship with or a relationship with. They put ads in magazines, on web sites and ask friends to hook them up. Some of these men are sincere, but there are those who are looking for prey. These are the ones you have to be on point with. It is very important that in the beginning of a relationship with a prisoner that you don't reveal if you're lonely also. The vulture will smell blood with that statement and similar statements by you. You have to be very cognizant of what you say and how you say it. It is best to state that you're in a shaky relationship and you do not mind just being friends. Give him something to fight for and don't give in or be a sucker for love as soon as he says he is falling in love with you or send you a beautiful poem. Keep your guards up and constantly test his sincerity. A prisoner can only hide the real him but for so long. Nine out of ten times, he doesn't know what love is and he did not write the poem. It is on you to constantly poke holes at his sincerity and see if he can whether the storm. If he is truly sincere then he is going to welcome your challenge and rough it out to prove to you just how sincere he truly is.

If you have children then he should be interested in your children just as much as he is interested in you. A sincere prisoner knows and understands that your children are an intricate part of you and are your pride and joy. I am not stating that he should want to adopt your children outright. However, he should try to develop a relationship with them as much as he does with you. His interest in your children should be a show and tell about his sincerity in developing a sound, long term relationship with you. If he calls and never asks to talk with the children then take note. If you decide to pay him a visit, bring your children and see how he interacts with them. See if he chooses to play cards with them or get a pen and paper to draw or write with them. See if he spends more time hugging and kissing you on the visit then he does building with the children. Every sincere man in prison loves the innocence of a child because he understands that he can harness that innocence and give that child viable information, especially if your child is male. Something in a conscious sincere prisoner kicks in when building with a man child. He knows he has an obligation to impart the correct information to that man child that will keep him from entering the prison system. If he does not take a sincere interest and grow to love your children, he is not sincerely interested in you and he will never love you sincerely. Beware of those prisoners that act like they're interested in developing a relationship with your children. This is a weak ploy to get you to think he is sincere and to get you to think this man is really interested in your children. Don't fall for that trick. Sincere interest in your child will show in the long term consistency, not just in the beginning of the relationship when he is trying to pull you.

Now, I have to be a little critical on the ladies. There exists a large number of females that stick with their man while he is incarcerated for ten, twenty and more years. Then when the prisoner is released, shortly thereafter, it is a breakup between the two. I have heard of a hundred times or more of how brother comes home and the female who stood by him, does not even see him until days, weeks and sometimes months after he is released. How does he come home and get with his baby's mother or old girlfriend? Now, I am not justifying their behavior but there are always two sides to a coin. What type of relationship did they hold while the prisoner was incarcerated? There are many females that enable negative behavior by prisoners. What do I mean? Well, it is no secret that drugs exist in prison. There are females that bring brothers drugs to prison, putting their own freedom in jeopardy, their children's welfare in harm's way and adding to the destructive behavior of their husband or boyfriend. Then they cry and complain about how this no good so and so came home and got right back into the drug game or how he got turned out on heroin or crack. Where is the personal responsibility on the female's part? What is going through that female's head that she thinks that she can supply him with illegal drugs for years and then think he is going to come home and do the right thing?

Prison can be a learning experience and surely has the ability to turn a man's life around especially if he has a good positive woman by his side holding him down. There also exists many females that do large amounts of time with a prisoner and never push him to correct his ways; never look to address his negative behaviors. I know brothers who have been in prison for over fifteen years and do not have a GED. Females have to recognize the power they have over their spouse when he is doing time. Do you know how many prisoners would leave the prison system with at least their GED if their spouse would demand that they get it by using packages, visits, letters and even phone calls against them? By letting their spouse clearly know that they are going to pull back in those areas if they don't put more effort and time in acquiring their GED.

There are a lot of programs in prison. Some are voluntary and some are mandatory. Programs are all good compared to spending time watching television, working out or playing games. If your child spent ninety percent of his time on the basketball court and with his play station, how would you feel? What are his chances of coming to prison? So, why do you accept this type of behavior from your spouse that is already incarcerated? You must demand that he get involved with programs while incarcerated. Not only demand it but make him prove it to you by talking to you about his program participation length. He can send you copies of his certificates once he completes these programs. Never allow him to tell you that he has taken all the programs there are. Maybe if he is in a camp that could be possible; however, if he is in a maximum security or a medium security facility in the New York State Department of Corrections, that is nearly impossible. There is always a wide variety of programs he can get involved with that will assist in his chances of getting him home, keeping him home and being a successful citizen. If he is adamant about there not being any programs in his facility, then he can always go to his correction counselor and request a program (education) transfer. If you are married to a prisoner you have the ability to call his correction counselor and talk to him about your husband's institution's record, his program needs and behavioral adjustment. You should always have the phone number to the facility your spouse is in and the name of his correction counselor.

Females must take an active role in their man's mental development while incarcerated if she truly desires for her spouse to come home a changed man. Of course, romance and chivalry plays a role in maintaining any relationship whether it is one being held by incarcerated couple or a couple in the free society. However, incarcerated couples have more obstacles and challenges to overcome, especially if there are children involved. This is why effective positive communication is so important. Visits are an excellent avenue to really gauge your man's sincerity in developing a relationship with you and developing himself because like the saying goes, "The eyes are the windows to the soul." It is on you to talk to him and question him about what he wants to do when he is released. Look in his eyes; your woman's intuition will kick in. If he comes down on every visit and plays cards you can basically assess what he is doing with his time inside the prison. It is not a good look if he is more concerned with what is going on in prison than he is with getting out of prison. Females should always pay attention to detail on all levels of communicating with a prisoner. The same energy and watchful eye put into visits should be applied with letter and phone calls. Females should always maintain a level of positive motivation for their spouse in letters, on the phone and during visits. These are the only avenues of communication for an incarcerated couple and must be utilized to the fullest.

A man that is doing time who does not have a plan is destined to come right back to prison. If your man refuses to plan then you can bet his plan is to fail upon his release. So you are wasting your time doing time with him. If the two of you are not working together, creating a plan of success then what is the relationship going to produce? There has to exist between the both of you a realistic outlook for the future.

Realistically, in today's society there needs to be a steady flow of income coming in the home to provide basic necessities. If there is no food, clothing and shelter realistically what kind of relationship can sustain under those conditions? Women are already dealing with enough in society. They do not need to be taking on an extra burden that is not going to produce anything good. I have noticed that a large number of females come to realize during the relationship that their spouse is not really about anything. Yeah, he may look good, nice and buff and hit them off with a couple of smooth lines to make them feel good, but he is not adding to her betterment and is financially draining her and wrecking her emotionally. She feels committed to stick it out because somewhere in her twisted thinking she feels that she can change him. Let me express something to all females who share these same thoughts. First of all, the only thing you should be totally committed to is you and your children. A prisoner is only going to do to you what you allow him to do. If you allow him to play games and do his time day by day then that is what he is going to do and continue to do it as long as you allow it. If he does not show appreciation for your woman's worth, what are you sticking around for? You may have spent a lot of time, money and feeling on him and feel that you have invested too much to let go now, but that is exactly what you should do if his release plan is not together and he is not seriously utilizing his time to address his crime generative attitude. Yes, it is hard to let go, but letting go frees you up for future happiness. You cannot allow yourself to be stuck in a relationship that is headed nowhere quickly.

Ladies, it is not an easy feat to develop a relationship with a prisoner. You must protect yourself from being mistreated, taken advantage of and even being under appreciated. Your best protection is critical analysis, hard questioning and effective utilization of all avenues of communication. Never rush a relationship with a prisoner. Allow it to take its natural course of development. If the relationship is destined to develop, then let it flow on its own. Ladies, I cannot stress enough that you must pay attention to detail in your relationships. There will always be signs that will illustrate rather clearly what kind of individual you are dealing with; it is on you to pay attention to the signs and act accordingly when reading them.

CHAPTER SIX
The Visit by Keisha Jackson

Traveling to the Correctional facility that confines and restricts my husband is a long hard and enduring journey that I do not enjoy at all. Though I don't enjoy the journey it is one I have to endure to spend quality time with my husband. Once I am in his arms it makes the journey worthwhile and the thoughts of the horrid trip fades away until I board the bus back to return home. Let me give you some insight on my feelings, the procedures, and encounters I go through and observe while under-taking this horrific journey.

Purchasing a ticket in advance where the prices fluctuate regularly makes the wait to board the bus quicker. They have two lines; one for pre-paid ticket holders, which is long but bearable, and one long line that seems to never end for people to purchase a ticket. Before boarding this bus called "Prison Gap" one has to step up to a van first. There you have to show your pre-paid ticket and identification. You can also get roles of quarters and purchase water, blankets, and candy before boarding the bus. After my first encounter with the prison Gap bus I learned to purchase these things and other material necessities for my journey in my neighborhood before the trip. Because the prices are exuberant and quality is not at its best. After waiting in the cold for hours, I am then being transported to board another bus due to unclean, mechanical problems, broken seats, broken monitors, and no heat. I decided not to take Prison Gap again due to the horrid service.

I am getting ahead of myself; let me start from the beginning. Once I tell my husband I am coming to visit on a certain date both of us are delighted and anxious for that date to come. The night before the visit I pack for our son and me gathering clothes, food, and other necessities. If I have a package for my husband, I send it up ahead of time to avoid extra baggage to travel with. I have seen many people with babies, packages, and luggage struggling to see their loved ones. This is a sight I avoid to experience. I live in Queens, NY so I have to travel to Manhattan to catch the bus upstate. Usually I try to get a ride or catch a cab to Manhattan. This way I can leave home at a certain time and the wait outside for the bus is not that long. I have seen many mothers, fathers and grandmothers, and children wait outside in harsh weather waiting to board the bus which can take up to three hours. Traveling with our son I try to find some sort of shelter to avoid the elements. Finally, the bus arrives and everyone boards. My last visit I decided to try another bus to get better service. Once on the bus, fare is collected and announcements are made on how one should conduct themselves on the bus, introduction of the driver and bus coordinator, the different facilities drop off that will be made, the last course of business is prayer then we begin our six hour ordeal on the road. On the new bus it is better than Prison Gap even though we had problems with the heat and the television monitor. There wasn't any central heat so it caused the bus to feel cold even with the uncomfortable bus seats the ride was still better than the other bus. I learned to do as others catching cat naps on the way upstate. The bus makes two or three stops along the way for passengers to use the bathroom, stretch their legs, smoke a cigarette, or grab a quick snack. I occupy myself by catching cat naps, having conversations with our son, or mostly thinking about my husband's loving arms.

Once we reach upstate, the bus driver proceeds to let passengers off at the facility they are visiting, telling them to enjoy their visit and he will be back to pick them up after the visit. In the upstate region you may have eight or nine facilities in a forty five minute radius.

When it is our turn to exit the bus we walk into a little mobile looking house. I instruct my son to go brush his teeth, use the toilet and take a quick wash up at the "slop sink" in the small bathroom that many people wait on line to utilize the "slop sink". Slop sink is just one of the many subtle dehumanizing techniques some facilities incorporate to foster low morale in visitors. What is a Slop Sink? Sounds like something pigs enjoy and utilize. While our son is dealing with his physical refinement and changing his clothes, I prepare him a cup of orange juice and a cup of oodles of noodles I purchased on the way upstate. The facility supplies the hot water I use to prepare the Oodles of Noodles. Then I proceed to sign in to visit my husband. I don't want to be one of the first to sign in fearing the officers will terminate our visit early if the visiting room gets too crowded. Once signed in I have an option of leaving a package as well. I have seen many people trying to leave lots of food items, clothes and shoes for their loved ones. Once called to the table visitors are told to put the items on the table while the officers sort through them and determine what an inmate can have and what he can't have. Items the inmate can't have the visitor has to take them back home or give them away. One time, I had to leave cooked refrigerated meats at the facility – the officer informed me they had to be package a certain way. I couldn't bring them back home for the fact they would have spoiled by time I reached back home. I also had to take back deodorants due to the officer stating that it had alcohol in it. Another time I had to take home coffee mugs even though they were plastic. The officer told me that type of mug he has a hard time passing so it is not allowed. Mind you there exists a departmental directive #4911 that governs approved and disapproved items in the facility. However, when bringing a package to a facility the items being approved are determined by the officer's attitude of the day. Yet, another dehumanizing technique utilized to make visitors feel powerless. After giving what is allowed I put the rest of the things in my issued locker and proceed to freshen up, change my clothes and use the bathroom in the small lavatory with the infamous "slop sink".

I then join our son at the table and drink a cup of tea while we wait to be called to visit my husband. After my tea and still waiting to be called I sometimes walk outside and smoke a cigarette thinking to myself the hell I have to go through just to see and hold my husband and how I long for the day he will be released out of this dreadful place. I also wonder while looking at the small buildings that make up the prison compound, wondering which one of the buildings my husband will walk out of – if he knew I was looking – or if he could see me. I go back inside the small mobile house making sure our belongings are secure in the issued locker. While waiting to be called, mothers are still getting their children and themselves together for their visit with their loved ones. While still waiting, I remember I have to get a paper bag for my belongings. I always have to take my bra and jewelry off to avoid the metal detectors. Once inside the visiting room I am able to put my bra and jewelry back on in the bathroom. Finally our number is called.

As I walk with my son to the main building I see some of the visitors that went before me walking back to the mobile home...some angry, some crying...some disappointed from being turned away. Later on during the bus ride home they explain out loud the reason they could not see their loved one. Some reason I heard were that did not enough identification, hair pins holding hairstyles in place and the worst they failed a random drug search in which nothing was found. One woman was accused of having cocaine residue on the bottom of her shoe and couldn't visit until the next 48 hours. State policy also states that if reason to believe you have illegal contraband (drugs) or came into contact with illegal contraband you must wait off facility grounds in the cold until the bus comes back after visiting hours. I tend to hold my breath hoping that the officers find no fictitious reason to turn me away without seeing my husband for some crazy unfair reason.

Once we enter the main building and our numbers are called, we go to a desk where we sign in again and show our ID. I then instruct my son to take off his coat and shoes as I do the same. We place them on a table for the officers to inspect. I also give them the paper bag that holds my jewelry, money, locker number disk and my bra to inspect. Can you just imagine the dehumanizing and powerlessness a female visitor experiences by relinquishing her under garment to a strange man to be inspected? Things they don't allow us to bring in they hold and place in another bag we are told we can get back after the visit. We then have to walk through the metal detector in which we were fortunate enough to pass through without setting it off. The officers then ask us to hold out our hands and place a stamp on the back of it. I think to myself, me and my son are being treated as prisoners instead of visitors to a prison. This is identical to a procedure slaves went through in the middle passage. Putting my child through all of this takes a toll on my mental. However, we both keep our minds clear and on our main goal which we are becoming closer to seeing our loved one.

We then wait for an iron automatic gate to open while putting our shoes and coats back on. The gate slowly opens and we proceed to the other side. Once on the other side more officers await us asking to see our stamped hands. We are also told to give our paper passes to the officers in the visiting room. We then walk outside towards another gate that we wait to hear the buzz to another gate to open so we can walk through. Once through this gate we walk down a walkway to another building.

Finally, we are in the visiting room and we walk to the front desk handing the officer our pass. The officer then instructs us what table to sit at. As we walk to our table, I look around at the little dismal play area for the children. The room is small and crowded with tables, chairs and vending machines. I instruct our son to stay seated as I walk into the bath room to put my bra back on and go to the vending machine to purchase our family something to drink and a few blocks with numbers on it that is utilized to take pictures. I then sit and wait for that wonderful moment to see my husband walk into the visiting room.

The longer it takes, I begin to get nervous and restless not wanting anything to go wrong in terms of not being able to see my husband. I notice other people waiting sensing they are having the same anxiety attack as I am. Finally, my husband walks into the visiting room walking to the officers asking which table. As I watch him, I begin to smile along with our son getting butterflies in my stomach. He turns around and we can't take it anymore, jumping up walking towards him getting our family hug on. He then holds me in his arms, kisses me lightly making me feel safe, warm, secure and making me feel like after riding and walking through hell everything is alright now.

At this point in our union we have developed the ability to block everything out. It's just our family in our own world until an officer comes by saying to him sit up, or instructing us to move our legs a certain way or just coming by our table to disrepute our diving serenity during our precious family visit. It is as if some officers get their rocks off disturbing and disruption family visits or they drive off of this illusion sense of power they assume during visiting hours.

Richard Jackson

I recall one visit I went without our son it was warm that day so we were allowed to go outside in a confined area that held limited tables with chairs attached. As I was basking in the warm rays of my husband, I noticed people walking in circles. It really amused me watching them walk around in circles in that small confined area. I inquired of my husband what are they doing. How crazy it looked walking around in circles like that. He explained to me about cattle be herded in a controlled environment. I thought it was ludicrous and did not want to participate in such an act.

On another visit he asked me to walk with him. I thought to myself hell no for half of a second, but the truth of the matter is that it is hard to refuse my husband. We began to walk, holding hands, talking laughing in that constricted circle. I then understood. We were so in tune with one another vibes it didn't appear we were walking in circles. The officers, the facility, the tall gates, the bob wire and everything else no longer existed. It was just me and my husband. The circle became a long beautiful path we walked down embraced in one another, enjoying one another. Once you make yourself aware of the mental tricks and games that are in place to hinder the bond between families under the guise of "Corrections." You empower yourself to see them for what they are and you can truly enjoy a visit to the fullest. The officers shouting outside times was up brought us back to reality – the reality that we can escape mentally.

When we are in the visiting room we are in our own world shutting everything and everyone out except the love we share for one another – nothing else matters at all until a loud demanding voice yells, "Count Time." My husband then stands as all inmates do and visitors remain seated in order for the facility to count. He always positions himself behind me during this time and starts to massage my shoulders. His touch makes me feel so nice at times I wonder what he is thinking during this time. What makes him want to massage me? Is it more for him than me? Does he get anything out of it? Or is it all for my pleasure? I mean to ask him this one day. After reading this, I await his answer. When our visit comes close to ending I feel so sad, empty and lonely inside. I want to just grab him and run out of that dreadful place with my husband but I cannot. The officers, the guns, the gates, the barbwire and that horrible bus just won't allow me. I hate leaving my husband in that place leaving without him is leaving a part of me that place. When the visit is over I want to cling to him for dear life.

I always try to be the last on line so I could keep him in my sight letting him know over and over I love him. Even though he tells me to go I see him watching me as well with pain in his eyes. It hurt to leave my husband behind in that place. It hurt so badly. Once the officer closes the door blocking our view from one another I try not to cry while a knot grows in my throat. I wait until the officer instructs us to walk through the gate with our passes. We then pass through more officers showing our passes and stamped hands. Back by the metal detector to collect our belongings we couldn't bring in. Then I have to go to a desk to pick up a package that my husband left for me to carry out those walls. Back to the mobile house to get our things out of the locker, and hand the metal locker disk back to the officer who unlocks the locker for you. Back to that dreadful bus to begin the journey hundreds of miles away from my husband. As the bus pulls away from the facility I watch and watch hoping to catch a glimpse of my husband wondering if he could still see me.

The bus makes a couple of stops on the six hour ride back home; picking up people from different facilities that we previously dropped off. The bus makes various stops on the return trip for people to get dinner which usually consist of KFC, 7 Eleven, or Mickey Dees. The journey home is full with a variety of mixed emotions shared by all. The sadness is so thick it is in the air. Some are silent, some are chaotic, some are frustrated, some are even crying and some will never board a bus upstate again. I focus on my husband in silence; remembering his words of strength and his gentle touch that stills embrace me. I drift off here and there for a couple of cat naps. The ride seems so much longer going back. We finally reach Manhattan at about 10:30pm or later. Our son and I grab our belongings. I grab his hand. At times he lets go of my hand offering to take some of our belongings from me speaking on how he misses his father. I respond, "me too." We pass derelicts, the dope heads, the homeless and search for a cab. Finally we catch one. When I don't take our son I do this alone. I tell the cab driver "Queens please" full of sadness hoping I make it back in time to receive a call from my husband; most of the time I do not. When we reach the house we are too tired to eat so we take turns showering. After the shower my son tell me, "Peace my Queen, I love you goodnight." I respond, "Peace, my young King. I love you." He knows and understands that his father is the King. I then open the package from my husband, look through our pictures, read one of his many letters to myself, think of him until I fall to rest still feeling his warm embrace and his lips; seeing his beautiful smile and those eyes of his so full of love for his family. I despise everything I have to go through to get back in my husband's arms. But I find myself dealing with this hell over and over again. I have no choice due to the fact I need to be in my king's warm, strong embrace so hell I endure until he is home with his family where he belongs.

CHAPTER SEVEN
Conversation between God and a Prisoner

God: My son, I have been observing you very closely for some time now and it is time we have a heart to mind conversation.

Prisoner: Thank you, for taking out the time to converse with me. I appreciate your guidance and protection during my many years of incarceration.

God: There is no need to thank me. I have an unconditional love for all my creations. I am not taking out time, I am making time. For, I made time so that my greatest creation cannot live hastily, be organized and use time as a timeline in achieving perfection.

Prisoner: There is so much in my life that I need answers to that I do not know where to start. My life has been so full of ups and downs, changes and turn-arounds.

God: My son, your life has been no different than the other eight billion of my greatest creations. Do you dare tell me you are a different? You are my creation living on earth under my care and guidance. Your decision in life moved you up and down; your relationship with the world put you through changes and turned you around.

Prisoner: Yes, my Savior, I understand your wisdom; pardon self for attempting to be other than what you planned for me to be. What I meant to elaborate on is that it is difficult for me to initiate a line of questioning even though I seek many answers.

God: You have always been a very, very intelligent person. Please be mindful that I bestowed your intelligence on you. So as the saying goes, "Keep it real with me." But my son more than anything else, keep it real with yourself because it is you that you have to sleep with at night and it is you that you must live with during the day.

Prisoner; I am being sincere with you My Father.

God: My son, I made you in my image, you are me and I am you. You should have no difficulty in asking me anything. You don't have difficulty talking to your Homeboys, you don't have difficulty talking to females over the phone or in letters, and you don't have difficulty requesting packages, visits or money orders. So why do you have difficulty conversing with your Supreme Father?

Prisoner: WOW! You sure have a way with words and you continuously refuse to allow me to hide or hinder myself from being that special creation that you intended for me to be. So, I am digging deep and there is one question that has been heavy on my mind for the better part of these two decades and change that I have been incarcerated. The question is very simplistic in its essence. Why? Why me? Why lock me up half of my teens, all of my twenties and all of my thirties and now chipping away at my forties?

God: Well, my son for someone who was having difficulty initiating a line of questions, you sure summoned up three rather quickly. You are correct, your question is rather simplistic in its essence. So, I will make the answer very simple; because you chose the life you lived! I created all mankind with unique talents that specifically define them. You chose to ignore your God given talents and run the street. I gave you Allah, Jesus, Buddha, Jah, Elijah and many walks of life that had the power to make you live a right and just life but you chose your god. Man's manufactured God, "The Dollar Bill." Your pursuit of man's made God, took out of your God-conscious state of mind and had you acting like a savage in the pursuit of happiness. Now that same man that had you chasing his god has convicted you of a crime and sentenced you to life in prison. You ask me why when you should be asking yourself why you left the flock. All the many years you have spent in prison is of your own doing. There is no one to blame but yourself. Seeking why? Does not change your condition or erase your previous actions.

Prisoner: I realize that it was my choices that brought me to prison. I also take full responsibility for my actions. I recognize holistically my actions as a youth were reckless and irresponsible but even after digesting your answer it's still hard for me to understand.

God: My son, I know you understand why because I didn't create mankind to take responsibility for their actions without understanding. Did you ever think about the man you unmercifully took the life of, his family and his inability to breathe for the last two decades and change? Your first question is why; so that you can bring a balance to your life that has always been there. You have learned enough and developed mentally over the years of your incarceration. Your first question should have been along the lines of. How can I forgive you taking one of my most valuable creations: How can you make atones with the victim's family? You must rid yourself of selfish thoughts and actions.

Prisoner: Am I truly a selfish individual? Because I have lay awake hundreds of nights to the wee hours of the morning with tears running down my face. Trying to put pieces together that just would not fit no matter how much I forced them. Can you give me a little break and maybe a little empathy? Of course, I have thought about the man's life that I took and I am deeply remorseful. I have made sincere attempts to make amends with the victim's family and atone for my negative actions. I think about his family especially his children that had to grow up without a father. I know it is extremely hard for them. I think about his wife who was forced to raise five children by herself, his mother that experienced that hardest pain a mother can endure which is burying her child. I think about his siblings that had to grow up without their brother's protection, guidance or love. Oh, yes, I have contemplated these aspects to a large degree over the many years of my incarceration. I am aware, fully aware that the sleepless nights will never come to an end. My past actions will haunt me forever. More than anything else I will forever seek the answer to why? Maybe there is no exact answer or maybe the answer lay deep within me or just maybe the answer will come with my very last cry.

God: I have stood in your corner all of your life even when you denied my existence, even when you refused to prostrate yourself before me. I stood by you at your weakest times in life. I gave you courage when in your heart you wanted to give up. I protected you from racist police, protected you when you were in knife fights and when you chose dishonorable friends. I kept your locker and your stomach filled when many around you had nothing. You seldom thanked me or ever truly gave me your total faith, but I maintained my faith in you throughout this ordeal mainly because I witnessed something in you that you have yet to recognize yourself.

Prisoner: I can understand me having to pay my debt to society for taking another man's life and for all the negative decisions that I made; that simultaneously hurt many lives but why does my family and loved ones have to suffer along with me? They did not do anything to warrant the pain and heartache in standing by me all of these years.

God: Now you are asking unselfish questions that illustrate you're truly special as a developing man. That is one of the hardest for my creations. Not only to learn but to understand as well. Everything in my universe vibrates – everything moves. This categorically means that nothing stands still, nothing is alone. Everything has a direct effect or indirect effect on everything else. Your family and loved ones are a part of you as you are a part of them. Your actions and your actions alone have caused them to suffer along with you. The sooner my creation realizes that no man is an island and what one man does affects the whole, the universe will be a much more peaceful place in which mankind can live in harmony. Then and only then will my creation truly understand, "Heaven on Earth."

Prisoner: I have endured a great deal during these many years of my incarceration and I truly honor and thank you for giving me strength when I became weak but I have to ask you why have you made my incarceration so difficult? Granted I have grown intellectually tremendously. My moral foundation is solid and I also feel that I have a purpose in life. However, the loneliness, the pain, the feelings of hopelessness really consumes me at times. Don't you think that I have suffered enough?

God: First and foremost, my son, I do not put my creations through more than they can single-handedly bear. Your incarceration has been difficult. I have made you witness death, I have made you witness and feel racism, I have made you feel the bite of solitude, I have made you feel and experience difficulties that have killed and crippled other men. Don't look at the difficulties and hardships that you have encountered. Look at the man these difficulties and hardships have shaped and molded. The racism you experienced gave you the motivation and fortitude to accomplish things you never thought you could do. The solitude assisted you in introspection and analyzing everything around you rather adequately. The witness of deaths instills in you your need to save lives and contribute to rebuilding your community. Difficulties in one's life are not impediments to a better life but temporary obstacles that one must overcome in his pursuit for success. Success is not measured by monetary gain. I measure success by one's good deeds in life. Your experience with difficulties and hardships has put you on course to accomplishing a lot of good deeds in life. Success is in your hands, you just have to recognize it for what it is. Not for what you perceive it to be.

Prisoner: Yes, my Lord. I have to agree with you. I once read that, "Truth crushed to the earth will rise again." I have taken full advantage of my time incarcerated. Granted the beginning was filled with a lot of misguided aggression and I have stumbled once or twice. However, I humbly state that I feel my good deeds tremendously outweigh my bad transgressions. I do understand that you have a special task for me and I am prepared to fulfill it. I know you are very busy so I am not going to hold you up too much longer. I just have one more question for you. When will you grant me the opportunity to be free? It is then and only then that I can truly effect change in my community and utilize all that learning during my many years of incarceration.

God: As you know, I knew the questions you were going to ask before you asked but I allowed you to vent and express yourself so that this conversation could be enlightening as well as cathartic. You have come a very long way since your incarceration and I am proud of your development. However, you still have some miles to travel. As I previously mentioned you are on the right course. You have asked when I will give you opportunity to be free. My son you have always been free. Being free is not your problem or any of my creation's problems. It is what you do with your freedom that has become the problems in life. I cannot give you a time and date to your physically freedom because that must be worked for, not handed out; but I can tell you that your physical freedom will be given to you just at the precise time. All that is required of you is that you stay ready so that you never have to get ready for your eventual freedom!

CHAPTER EIGHT
Evolution of Struggle

Time is gripping my area and pressing on my exterior
Just about to grasp and penetrate my placenta.
Feeling the aura of Goree Island.
Millions of us broken like a Stallion
Thousands of Black Men, Woman and Children
Traumatized by the capture, torture and stripping of their culture.
Nowhere to turn but in
Building up the rage and frustration
Only to have our development arrested by lack of recreation
On Master's plantation.
Working from sun up to sun down.
Now we just sit around and give each other
A POUND!
Mothers crying while their precious babies are dying
And nobody asks why.
Because the blood never runs dry from the lashes on our back
Or the scars on our hearts and the shackles on our brains
That drains and sprains our sanity.
Then freed into reconstruction without a clue
Of what the f*** a people should do!
Diagnosed with a vacant esteem?
Now can you tell me what the hell that is supposed to mean?
Living a dream of finally being physically free.
Only to later be hung from a tree.
Never giving up or becoming bitter because of our inherited
Third class citizenship.
Because we did learn how to read a little "bit".
Giving religion our total faith to bring us up out of this place.
AME gave us a link to our spirituality,
But nothing towards our forsaken reality.
Not to knock it but who cares about what's in your pocket when your children
Don't have eye sockets

They cannot see the foresight to understand their civil rights
Up you might race!
Clear the tears from your face.
Understand your ancestors are Kings and Queens
Who lived dreams?
The Civil Rights Movement ushered in a new consciousness,
But was met with vicious, malicious racism.
In a country that no longer need our labor,
So they took us for a ride on the transportation of legal genocide.
But we prevailed to kill Jim Crow,
But who knew we would lose so many heroes.
Now I don't have to ride on the back of a bus
Because in God we trust!
I can finally eat at the same food counter
But I better not turn my head or my family just might find me dead.
My children can finally go to school with others…we are truly brothers?
I figure…but behind my back you are calling them Nigga.
Why can't no one understand my frustration and aggravations?
Continuously dealing with the subtle oppression.
Life has never been so d*** hard!
Dealing with these situations
Without a God.
You would think that life would get easier from transition to transition;
I finally see that we must look WITHIN
To truly WIN!
Now Blacks are stereotyped with an inept criminality.

New York Police are getting outrageous with police brutality.
Makes you want to question who are you?
But no matter what the evolution of our struggle must CONTINUE!

My personal views on the state of African Americans in the areas of
politics, economics, employment and community empowerment is that
we are in a very critical situation and our condition will get extremely
worse if we do not begin to re-evaluate our state from an Afro-Centric
Perspective.

Historically, we have always been a very intelligent race of people. Starting from the first dynasty 3100 BC, there was a great Egyptian King name Aha (Menes). He unified upper and Lower Egypt at a time when it was logistically and ideologically near impossible. . He accomplished this mainly by instituting a centralized government that spread over all providence's and constituted kingdoms. Aha's unique ability to satisfy the people's needs brought about the kind innovations and stability in his administration that not only provided a solid foundation for the first Egyptian dynasty, but also the economic and social conditions necessary to sustain the Egyptians for many more dynasties.

In looking at the accomplishment and outstanding display of organizational skills under Aha's rule we see that this was politics in its earliest application from an Afro-Centric perspective. In 2008, we see that the African American experience in the field of politics is in total contradiction to King Aha's example; Instead of elected officials rallying around a collective African American agenda that will unify African Americans, we see division and unrest amongst them. Aha came from amongst the people, articulated the thoughts, desires and needs of the people. To say the least, these characteristics are in short supply among our current elected officials. Our elected officials must start being held accountable for their actions when making decisions that directly affect the people. We can no longer accept or afford for our elected officials to continue making back door deals and not being an adequate voice for the people. They must know that if they do not represent the people's aspirations 100% then they will be removed from their positions. Politics can be defined as "the art and process of gaining, maintaining and using power." (Apter, David. 1977 Introduction to Political Analysis). This definition of politics has yet to have its full impact on the majority of African Americans. Because we witness election after election the small turn out among African Americans. We are the very first to complain about social ills but the very last utilize our voting power.

If we truly want to change our social conditions and civil statuses then it is imperative for us to understand the power of our vote. Malcolm X stated "the ballot or the bullet" because he thoroughly understood the power that 30 million plus Black Americans had in their vote. Political power is essential for the uplift and stability of any race. We, as African Americans, must begin to see politics from an African worldview and look into our glorious history for direction and answers to fit our present state. In doing this, we must ask ourselves, why did that Dutch South Africans deny the original South Africans from voting during the Apartheid regime? The fact that Black and Latino communities have very little or no control over the institutions that determine their quality of life is a major part of the reason we do not have a percentage of people employed. Employment is an enormous problem in the Black and Latino communities that has a devastating impact on our youth. Let's start by looking at the root cause for unemployment and underemployment among Black and Latino people. The root cause, in my overview, lies within the education system. American society is bent on a person's qualification being determined by a piece of paper (degree) which is acquired by successfully completing levels of the American education system. If an individual cannot successfully complete the American education system and obtain a degree then his chances of acquiring a meaningful job that will enable him to provide a home, food and clothing for his family are slim to none.

The American education system did not originate to teach Black and Latino people and when we send our children to these schools they do not see themselves in the curriculum. By not seeing themselves in the curriculum they begin to lose interest and eventually drop out at alarming rates. Statistics show that fifty percent of African American high school students drop out. They drop out with attitudes, describing schools for suckers or that they can learn more on the streets. By dropping out of school they drop out of the work market and their chances of acquiring gainful employment drastically drop.

African Americans often interpret unemployment not as a problem of education but as a problem of being Black. This can be categorized as institutional racism. Institutional racism, in my opinion, is the worst kind of racism because if not combated with a strong mind it can reduce a person's self-esteem. Institutional racism is when an institution refuses to let an individual climb the corporate ladder (advance) on the sole basis of race. It is a known fact that a white man with a high school diploma can get a better job and make more money than a black man with a college degree. This is because we have been "relegated in a caste position in American society, and no Black or Latino, no matter who they know or his/her level of education or achievements, should expect to be accorded treatment equal to that of a white person." (Pinkney, Aphonso 1987 Black Americans).

Crime and drugs have become an employment relief for a large majority of our youth. Living in a society that categorizes success by material gain we see our youth yearning to want the materialistic things in life. With no jobs the only avenue left open to them to obtain these material items is either through crime or drug selling. Then we can clearly see why "25% of our young Black men between the ages of 20 and 29 are under the control of the criminal justice system."

Well over 3 billion dollars pour out of African American communities each year. This statistic shows that we are great consumers and have more purchasing power then most third world countries. A people that consumes as much as we do should have an economic base that can be utilized to benefit the growth and development of our children. "Economics is generally defined as the study and process of producing, distributing (or exchanging) and consuming goods and services." (Karenga, Maulana 1993 Introduction to Black Studies). If all we are doing is consuming then we are leaving out major parts of key economic stability such as producing studying and distributing. The principal reasons why African American economics is only consuming and leaving other key ingredients out of its recipe of successful economics, is because we are dealing individually and there is no power in individualism among a people. We must begin to pool our resources and practice cooperative economics. "The theory and practice of cooperative economics has an early history in the mutual aid societies in northern

Black communities, which pooled resources and dedicated themselves to social service and community development." (Harris, Abram 1936 The Negro Capitalist, Philadelphia: American Academy of Political Science). If we can begin to develop a system of cooperative Black economics then we can start to establish some solutions for 1) social changes 2) consumer unions 3) community repair 4) unemployment 5) crime/drugs 6) institutional racism and many other social ills that affect our communities. The reason why solutions can be established after we start practicing cooperative economics is because there will begin to be a large influx of money coming back into the African American community.

African Americans must also recognize the economic benefit in controlling the institutions that serve 50% of more of our people. For example, the New York State prison system grosses millions of dollars each year. It is populated by 85% Black and Latino prisoners in which 75% of them come from seven neighborhoods in New York City. By these statistics you can see that the prison institution serves specific communities but the benefits, which amount to millions of dollars a year, do not serve our deteriorating neighborhoods. We must begin to have a say so in all and any institution that serves our people from the hospitals to the courthouses. The economic relief that comes from the institutions that serve our people must serve us as well or we should mobilize and shut them down.

If we, as a people, begin to understand the importance of controlling the institutions that serve our people and determine the quality of our living conditions, then we can begin to understand what community's empowerment is all about. If we, as African Americans, wish to advance in this North American society we must have adequate input in the institutions that serve our people. Community empowerment, self-determination, and self-esteem are closely knitted together to produce a strong fabric. If we, as a people, are to truly empower ourselves we must first regain our high level of self-esteem. "Slavery was "legally" ended in excess of 100 years ago, but the over 300 years experienced in its brutality and unnaturalness constituted a severe psychological and social shock to the minds of African Americans.

Therefore, it is fair to say that slavery was a major contributor to the reduction of our self-esteem. In 2008, our self-esteem was so low that we hate ourselves. At one time in history, we loved ourselves and everything that we represented. Now we can no longer look at another black man and see our father or brother, we can no longer look at a Black woman and see our grandmother or little sister. This is because our mirror image has been substituted by a piece of aluminum foil. When you look into a piece of aluminum you see a distorted figure. We must begin to start loving each other and restore our mirror image values. How will we ever empower ourselves if we do not love ourselves and see ourselves as brothers and sisters?

Community Empowerment entails that a people become more community specific and understand that growth and development of a race of people lies in the hands of their ancestors. We are the ancestors of our up and coming children. If we wish for them to have the things that we could not obtain in our lifespans then it is our obligation to set the groundwork for empowerment. We must strongly understand that empowerment does not come overnight. When there is an organized or unorganized plan to exchange power form one party to another there will be conflict. "If you are cut down in a movement that is designed to save the soul of a nation, then no other death could be more redemptive." (King, Coretta Scott. 1987 The Words of Martin Luther King, Jr.).

In re-evaluating our present state in the areas of politics, employment, economics and community empowerment, I contend that in order for African Americans to be successful in these fields we must begin to address them non-traditionally. History shows us that the traditional methods and solutions do not work for us. If we continue to address our problems traditionally, which is euro-centrically, we will be a forgotten race of people 20 years from now. We must not lump Black and Latino issues together. Even though we have a common oppressor in this country and around the world, Latinos have unique needs that can best be addressed by them. The question of language has left them somewhat at a disadvantage and their unique cultural expressions are often misunderstood. There is a great need for Latinos to develop a Latin agenda and for African Americans to recognize our common oppressor and to move in a collective direction.

In the field of economics African Americans must begin to create more jobs for our youth to cling to. We cannot continue to lose our youth to drugs, crime, prison or death because the economic stability of our community is so low. Jobs come from political power, "It would be relatively impossible and certainly unwise and irregular for national leaders to make political decisions without economic considerations. In fact, politics and economics are unavoidable linked on several levels." (Karenga, Maulana. 1993 Introduction to Black Studies). So once again we see how important it is for us to become politically aware and how important our vote is. Dedicated African American leaders can answer our cry for help if we just learn how to develop them to their maximum potential.

We must also keep in mind that a failure in any one of these institutions; politics, community empowerment, employment, economics will result in a high crime rate. In addressing these failures from a non-traditional approach our goal should be to empower these institutions with the ability to transform themselves from dysfunctional institutions to working community specific institutions that will address the specific needs of our communities from an Afro-Centric perspective.

CHAPTER NINE
Growing Pains & Strains

When one is enduring isolation in the form of New York State's Prison Industrial Complex, one has various and fluctuating degrees of emotions that have to be managed intelligently for optimal elevation.

The first emotion that must be addressed is anger! In psychological terms, anger is defined as, "an acute emotional reaction elicited by any number of stimulating situations, including threat, over aggression, restraint, verbal attack, disappointment, or frustration and characterized by strong responses in the autonomic nervous system." Now that we are working off of this solid (foundation) definition of anger. Let's see what the average prisoner does with it. I can only speak for myself and with my twenty-three years of observance confined in the New York State Department of Corrections. Anger is a very deadly emotion. It has the ability to blind one of all rational and intelligent thought. When one is confined; especially in a controlled environment with the same sex, deprived of many liberties and subject to dehumanizing techniques it can cause one's internal anger to outwardly explode like an atomic nuclear bomb.

I have come into direct contact with many prisoners that were sentenced to two, three, four years and because their anger was not tamed they spent fifteen to twenty or more years in prison and those were the lucky ones. The unlucky ones allowed their uncontrolled anger to lead them to an early death, finding themselves on the other side of a shank (knife) held by an equally angry contender. Being angry in prison, especially among individuals serving lengthy sentences is seen to be normal behavior amongst the general the population. That is one thing about prison life; one becomes accustomed to accept the abnormal as normal. A hell of a way to live. But what is even more ironic is that one must adjust to this abnormal way of thinking and living in order to survive and stay alive.

The Department of Corrections in New York State does offer prisoners with violent crimes and behaviors a therapeutic anger program called Aggression Replacement Treatment (ART). The ART program has some very good tenets to it when one is objective and seeking assistance to deal with his anger. I specifically appreciated the tenet dealing with "Moral Development"; this section of the ART program deals with a slew of scenarios that are very realistic. The scenarios are given to participants and they have to think their way through them, without acting in an angry and violent manner. All scenarios prompt angry emotions in one's self. So to think them out with rational thought is a task and a learning experience on how one can alleviate anger and act intelligently regardless of the situation one finds himself in. The scenarios foster "Moral Development". However, most prisoners do not take to the ART programs because it is a mandatory program for those with violent crimes, it is facilitated by prisoners and mainly because they are so caught up in their own wayward anger they do not (see) recognize the good in the state sponsored program.

I have learned to deal with my anger by trial and error. I thank God it was not too much error. My untamed anger at seventeen years of age caused me to take another human's life without regard for human life. Anger blinds, anger dumbs down, anger gives a false sense of bravado grandiose, anger also kills the real you. One who lives with anger lives with the devil and death. These people are magnets to destructive behavior and negative mind frames. The flip side about anger is that it can be utilized as an excellent self-motivational tool. I have witnessed prisoners so upset and angry with the unjust treatment they received from the Criminal Justice System that they lashed out by emerging themselves in the Law Library diligently. Learning and mastering the foreign language of law until they was able to free themselves and triumphantly correct the injustice that was bestowed upon them by the Criminal Justice System. I witnessed men that were extremely angry with themselves because they did not have a basic education. They did not allow their anger to dumb them down or impede their development as a growing man. They took their literacy decrement and raised it to unbelievable heights. It is really extraordinary when you can witness an individual with no formal education utilize his anger and achieve a GED, push on to an Associate's Degree, push further to a Bachelor's Degree and then accomplish the almost unbelievable under prison condition and acquire a Master's Degree. I take these amazing feats as true anger management.

I have learned over the years that misplaced as well as placed anger promulgate consequences. Being incarcerated in New York State Prison the negative consequences of one's misplaced anger can be very detrimental to one's livelihood. It is an environment that has a slippery slope downhill if one is not totally conscious of his action. I tend to always manage my anger so that I will be rewarded with positive consequences for my actions.

Anger is just one emotion that one confined to a state institution has to combat on a regular basis. Other emotions such as frustration, loneliness, helplessness and hopelessness are a few more emotions that can be very debilitating to a prisoner. Another ironic aspect of these emotions is that they all can lead to misplaced anger and eventually mushroom into a violent episode. So it is very important that a prisoner, especially one faced with doing a considerable amount of time, address his anger early in doing time. Efficient anger management is key to successfully doing time, accomplishing skills and acquiring one's freedom and returning to society a whole man instead of a bitter man thinking the world owes you (them) something.

The flip side of anger is that very sacred and treasured emotion called L-O-V-E. This is an emotion that the majority of prisoners have a very hard time discussing. Though there exists in New York State, programs addressing Drug Addiction, Anger, Domestic Violence, Sexual Deviance and a couple of others. There is not one state sponsored program that deals with LOVE. In my professional opinion as a prisoner, what will greatly assist in a prisoner rehabilitating himself is a clear understand of what love is and how to love. Love is taboo in prison because it is filled with so much testosterone and machoism. One who is living and shows sincere love and affection to his brother is seen as weak and is preyed on by others. But either doing short time or long time during every prisoner yearns to be loved and have spent many sleepless nights trying to figure out how they can obtain true love.

Okay, let's try to assemble all of this in its rightful place. Most prisoners entered prison deprived of love or never truly experiencing it or had never truly been loved themselves. Their perception of love is what they garnished through media, novels and some unhealthy relationships or word of mouth. I have met many men that thought love was receiving a 35lb package, love was obtaining a visit, love was someone accepting a collect phone call, and love was having sexual intercourse. Now these gestures might have a semblance of love but by far cannot be defined as complete love. Love is so much more than receiving. By no means am I an expert on love. In fact, I still have a way to go in truly understanding and incorporating the true essence of love into my life. The more one elevates himself in knowledge, wisdom and understanding, the more love begins to manifest itself. I have looked in a number of dictionaries and even in a psychological dictionary. All dictionaries connect love with sexual intercourse or sexual gratification. This is a conjecture that I totally disagree with because I have not experienced any sexual intercourse in over two decades. Also, how do you apply this sexual connotation to love with the same sex such as brother, sisters, best friends, etc? That's what's so unique about love; you cannot allow anyone to define it for you.

I have learned to love simply by allowing myself to be vulnerable. It may sound like an easy feat to most but for someone incarcerated, vulnerability means easy prey and open for pain, two sentiments that prisoners avoid with vigilance. I first started opening up myself to love and allowing myself to be loved by my nuclear family the prisoner mindset and a criminal mindset hold many similarities. When I was living in society yes I loved my family and they loved me more. The question is did I understand the love I had for my family? Better yet, did I appreciate it and reciprocate it? There exists a very unique flavor in true family love that can penetrate steel. My inability to see or appreciate my family's unconditional love was accelerated by my life sentence to prison. The isolation of prison life does one of two things. 1) Forces you to do some introspection, 2) Cause you to further your negative and destructive behavior. There's no fence, however, some can cleverly blanket what side they are truly on. My introspection brought it to light that my family truly loves me because here I am a young youth running wild, getting arrested and when I am in the court room facing the judge and I look back --- who's there! Family!

When I was sentenced to life and ready to give up on myself! Who was there giving me strength to hold on? Family! When I am upstate hundreds of miles away from home, who comes to visit me and gives me that hug I need but is scared to ask for? Family! When I feel like the walls are closing in and the air gets thin because I am surrounded by hate, rape and a host of characteristics that I could never appreciate. So I reach out to pick up the phone and call home who's on the other end to accept my collect call and be a true friend? Family! So I began to allow myself to be vulnerable. I allowed myself for the first time to be loved and it felt wonderful. I realized as Stephanie Mills said in one of her songs, "The Power of Love". I have learned that it is easier to live with love than with anger. An angry mind has no future because his anger leads him down dangerous roads, blinded, and dumbed down with a false sense of bravado. That will eventually lead into a dead END.

However, love is a door opener, it can heal, and it can bring you closer to God. But most importantly to me it brings peace and warmth to my existence. By no means am I preaching that all prisoners should be suckers for love. Number 1 Love hurts and like the saying goes, "there's a thin line between love and hate." However, every human being should allow themselves to be vulnerable for love because love has the ability to open one up to the world and see it for what it really is. When you don't allow yourself to love or be loved it's like walking through life with blinders on.

What I appreciate the most about loving and being loved is the communication level. That is the true indicator of love when you can express yourself freely without hang-ups. Once I opened myself up for love I created an avenue to let out the anger. You will be amazed at how much a sincere conversation with a loved one can do for you. Look at children and why it's so easy to love them because when you talk with them they are brutally honest they are vulnerable and they give you unconditional love. There is no mask with children what you see is what you get. Tell me what child you do not love and I will show you a child that reminds you of the part of you that you do not love. I love children to death and whenever I come in contact with that youth that reminds me of myself; I reach out to love him even more because I know first-hand that he needs love and that ability to free himself of those blinders.

I now love with ease and the easiness of my love allows people to see the beautiful person within me. They do not get stuck on that incarcerated man that murderer or any outward definition by society or stereotypes. A person that comes in contact with me will love me tomorrow because like that child, with me, what you see is what you get. Yes, I am now vulnerable but I am strong and my strength is in my ability to love and be loved. I am no longer afraid to show my vulnerability, my insecurities or my preconceived fears because the warmth and peace of love ushers me to share my true personality with others. In sharing my true personality I am able to receive beautiful people in my life. Even though I am in prison I can enjoy life, liberty and love just like any other citizen. My fluctuating emotions are managed intelligently and I am constantly striving for optimal elevation.

CHAPTER TEN
The Direct Relationship between Blacks, Latinos and the New York State Department of Corrections

My name is Richard R. Jackson and I have been incarcerated in the New York (NYSDOC) for twenty five years. When I entered the NYSCDOC, I was seventeen years old, very violent, no sense of direction and infatuated with street life and an inability to communicate rationally with others. I did not appreciate life or even respect life; which ultimately lead me to taking another man's life and being sentenced to seventeen and a half years to life in the year of 1986. Because of my long incarceration and knowledgeable learning experiences, I have come to understand and articulate the Direct Relationship between Blacks and Latinos living in specific communities and the New York State Department of Corrections; also the historical and social ramification that lead to this direct relationship. The consequences of this Direct Relationship has crippled communities, destroyed families, ruined lives and now have the state of New York economically depressed, crumbling from within because it promotes this Direct Relationship and chooses to spend "2.5 billion dollars annually. (Fischer, Brian. 2009, January 27) to incarcerate rather than sever the umbilical cord that inextricably links Black and Latino communities to the New York State Department corrections.

When I first entered the NYSDOC the full impact of my total incarceration did not hit me until a few years into sentence because I was still living with a street mentality, unconsciously I saw the NYSDOC as an extension of my community. Sadly enough, it was like a reunion of some sort because I knew the majority of the men I was incarcerated with. I was later to learn it was not a coincidence that my neighborhood was one of a few that was plagued with institutional failures that fed the NYSDOC this is why so many of us were familiar with one another. I did not know that my incarceration was linked to thousands of other Black and Latinos that originated in specific Assembly Districts located in New York City. I spent the first couple of years of my incarceration submerging myself in the prison culture despite these facts, subconsciously I knew that if I wanted to live through my term of incarceration I had to change my ways; specifically my attitude about life. I had no idea that I had developed an attitude that stated crime and violence was acceptable behaviors in my community. I would later learn that this attitude was inbred in me and shared amongst thousands of other Black and Latino prisoners because of social, political and economic conditions prevalent in our communities. In 1987, my mother shouldered the blame for my incarceration and attempted suicide. The fact that her baby boy was incarcerated at seventeen with a life sentence just was too much for her to bear. After this ordeal, I consciously sought out information to assist me in better understanding why I led the life I lived and chose to commit crimes in my community. Straddling the fence of better understanding the reasons for my incarceration and upholding my street reputation, I found myself in the middle of a prison riot in Coxsackle Correctional Facility that lasted four days. Afterwards, I found myself being transferred from Coxsackle to Green Haven Correctional Facility. I was one of three adolescents in an adult prison with a population of over two thousand prisoners. Back in those days it was common for an olde, more seasoned prisoner to take a young inexperienced prisoner under his wing (befriend) and school them on how to best utilize their time and be productive law abiding citizens upon their release. I was put under the wind of Eddie Ellis a very seasoned political prisoner. This was the beginning of a learning experience that would change the course of not just my life but the paradigm in which prisoners interacted with prison administration, community activist and legislators.

Eddie Ellis created a program called the Resurrection Study Group (RSG) in September of 1989 at Green Haven Correctional Facility. The focal points of the program were Leadership Development, Prison Problem Solvers and Community Development. The program model used non-traditional approaches to criminal and social justice issues that emphasized community empowerment. This is where my learning process began in terms of Black and Latinos into the criminal justice system and eventually the department of corrections. This was done by gathering and researching information dating back to the civil war. What was startling is that Blacks have been represented in the New York State prison system at a rate four to six times higher than their percentage in the New York State general population. However, they represent more than 85% of New York State's prison population. In analyzing the influx of Blacks and Latinos growth in the NYS prison system, I further learned that in the 1940s the NYS prison system was predominantly white, namely Irish and Italian. However, over a fifty year period of time the complexion of the prison system dramatically changed and is now incarcerating primarily Blacks and Latinos in an astronomically high numbers. Research by Owens, Charles (n.d) revealed that beginning "with an analysis of plantation life; the slave codes of 1690; the United States Constitution's definition of African people being equal to three-fifths of a human being." (P.1-14) All in which qualified slavery for 'Ahati N.N. Toure (2006) "a legal system that put into practice a two-tier system of criminal justice to be separately applied to Africans and Europeans; development of such a system laid the foundation for continuous mistreatment, exploitation and victimization of Africans (and later applied to Latinos) in New York State and across the country" (p.1) These historical facts coupled with deplorable social political and economic condition in Black and Latino communities along with "the rise of the Civil Rights movements lead to a rapid increase of Blacks and Latinos into the prison system as targeted individuals because of internal and group conflicts initiated by the Federal Bureau of Investigation Counter Intelligence program (cointelpro)". Hind S., Lennox (1978).

In learning these few facts, I began to understand that no individual act alone can account for the wide spread incarceration and major influx of Blacks and Latinos into the NYS prison system. By 1970, Blacks and Latinos numbers grew to the extent that they now became the majority of the population in the NYS prison system which resulted in a new political consciousness among Black and Latino prisoners, most of these prisoners where socially and politically active in their communities and who came from groups and organizations such as the Black Panther Party, Young Lords, 5% Nation, Black Muslims (N.O.I.), etc, because of the political consciousness of this new breed of prisoners and Blacks and Latinos becoming the majority of the NYS prison system resulted in a number of racial riots because Blacks and Latinos began to challenge existing racist policies that favored white prisoners and placed Black and Latinos in a subjugated positon. Racial riots and attacks against prison administration throughout the State of New York in many local jails an state prisons reached a boiling point in 1971 and expressed itself in the Attica uprising. The history of the Attica uprising is well documented; what is not documented is that the majority of men that survived Attica's uprising were transferred to two prisons in New York State; Eastern Correctional Facility and Green Haven Correctional Facility.

Eddie Ellis was one of the men who was transferred to Green Haven Correctional Facility. These socially and politically conscious prisoners moved forward in forging better conditions for Blacks and Latinos in the state prison system by the formation of a "Think Tank" in Green Haven Correctional Facility in 1972. Eddie Ellis and Larry White were pioneers in this Think Tank and they began to look at the prison system holistically and sought to answer what they termed the "Basic Question". "How is it that Black and Latinos together represent less than 28% of the general population of NYS, while at the very same time, they comprise 85% of the total state prison population, and over 75% of this total state prison population comes from New York City?" How can we account for this disproportionate representation? How did this happen? What are the future implications? In answering this basic question the Think Tank discovered some alarming facts that when I learned them, it changed my whole outlook on my incarceration and thoughts on Blacks and Latinos in prison.

The alarming facts of research revealed by Clines, Francis X. (1992) "that over 75% of the total state prison population comes from New York City, primarily located in predominantly Black and Latino communities which was identified as Assembly Districts 29, 31, 32, 33, 35, 40, 43, 51, 54, 55, 56, 57, 58, 68, 70, 71, 74, 75, 76, 77, 78, 79, 83. The overwhelming majority of these Assembly Districts come from specific jurisdiction referred to as the "seven neighborhoods"; Harlem,

South Jamaica, Bedford Stuyvesant, South Bronx, East New York, Lower East Side and Brownsville." (p. A1). All of the statistics and demographics revealed that there is a Direct Relationship between specific communities and the New York State prison system. This demographic clearly demonstrates that prisons have become institutions which now serve Black and Latino communities much the same as the church or schools. The Direct Relationship reveals that each feeds from and is sustained by the other; that a social, cultural, political and economic umbilical cord exists between the community and the NYS prison system; and that the revolving door syndrome of criminal recidivism is in fact this umbilical cord because of this link that is called, "The Direct Relationship". I learned that it is community specific, racial and cultural, the traditional or commonly accepted theories and methods of explaining and analyzing criminal and social justice problems were found to be misleading, inaccurate and counter-productive. Crime is socially defined and changes as social conditions and social leadership change. Since crime is more broadly defined in times of economic hardship and since this impacts greatest on inner city communities of color a deeper analysis had to be undertaken to more adequately understand and combat the Black and Latino experience in these specific communities outlined in the Direct Relationship.

I furthered learned that there exists what was termed as "Crime Generative Factors" (CGF) in these specific communities that represented the majority of the NYS prison population. These Crime Generative Factors are social, economic, political and infrastructural conditions that are prevalent in specific communities that generate crime, namely: institutional racism, family breakdown, miseducation, employment, drugs poverty and crime. These factors in themselves don't produce crime; they produce attitudes once faced with these factors on daily basis. These attitudes are termed "Crime Generative Attitude (CGA). These attitudes generate mindsets such as "I got to get mine," "Disregard for the law (norms)," "I am in this alone,"etc. These attitudes eventually lead into breaking the law, which leads to arrest and cumulating in one being incarcerated. In the Resurrection Study Group, I learned many ideologies and concepts to combat my Crime Generative

Attitude such as being community specific, my ethnic status, and a sense of community, self and community empowerment, reconciliation and others. The central theme of these concepts and ideologies was to address the individual offender by emphasizing the importance of personal responsibility. They defined the process by which each offender must undertake in a debt owed to the community. Moreover, that an offender with this knowledge has a personal responsibility to jam the revolving door of recidivism and impede the influx of Blacks and Latinos entering the NYS prison system in such alarming numbers.

Armed with this empowering and mind transforming information that clearly demonstrated that my community and many other Black and Latino communities are targeted for mass incarceration; I started to engage in developing community specific programs within the prison system. One of the first community specific program developments I was actively involved with was the Youth Assistance program (YAP). I was an integral participant of the team in 1988 to bring the YAP to Green Haven Correction Facility and other prisons through NYS. The YAP was non-traditional in regards to the scared straight program approach. The Scared Straight program applied the traditional approach in scaring the youth about incarceration. The YAP initiated a non-traditional approach by educating the youth about the demographics of the prison system and illustrating the Crime Generative Factors and the attitudes that they produce; Thus, giving the youth a knowledge base so that they can combat these Crime Generative Attitudes that so many of them possess. Throughout the years, I have been an instrumental part in tweaking many YAP throughout the state of New York inside the Department of Corrections. When incarcerated a Mid-Orange Correctional Facility, I was selected to be transported out of the prison to secure youth facilities and schools in Orange County, NY to talk to at risk youth and stare them straight as opposed to scaring them straight. What I learned most from talking to at risk youth about Crime Generative Factors and the Attitudes that they produces as well as the Direct Relationship is that we tend to underestimate the comprehension of our youth. Many of them grasp this knowledge rather quickly and was able to process it and make statement like, "they trapped me". Also out of the Think Tank evolved a Political Action Committee (PAC). This entity was composed of representative from established prisoner organizations and other concerned, social conscious prisoners at Green Haven Correctional Facility. The purpose, objective and main focus of the PAC was:

- To develop concepts and strategies for the creation of a new prison movement based up Non-Traditional Approaches to criminal and social justice issues.

- To support and encourage linkage between prisoner organizations and community based programs that seek improvement in criminal and social justice policies.

- To interpret criminal and social justice policies, to perform research and release findings and to develop community specific correctional program models.

- To set standards of personal development and achievements that empowers state prisoners to exercise responsibility.

- To act as a catalyst for change and to develop levels of communication between prisoners, their communities and the criminal justice system.

The PAC efforts led to annual Legislative Conferences held at Green Haven Correctional Facility. The primary purpose of these conferences was to provide a forum where communities most affected by the Direct Relationship could be afforded the opportunity to address prison administrative officials on issues of accountability and community input into the correctional process. The legislative conference bridged the gap between the community, prisoners, prison administration (state and local), and legislators for the first time in prison history, to address the "Basic Question" and to find effective solutions in dealing with this diabolical Direct Relationship. The central theme of all the legislative conference was to take an objective look at and consider not only the individual offender but the consequences incurred if we continue to ignore the effects of the social conditions in deprived communities. Also, that no society should expect to contain its problem of crime by way of longer prison sentences and punishment without considering the need to address the root cause of crime.

I played a major role in articulating non-traditional information at these legislative conferences, from heading workshops on definitive criteria's for parole to program proposals on youth specific programs within the prison system. Today almost twenty-one years after entering the Resurrection Study Group and where my learning experience began. I am facilitating the Resurrection Study Group here at Fishkill Correctional Facility as I did throughout the years in Green Haven, Woodbourne, Mid-Orange, Barehill and Clinton Correctional Facilities.

My learning experience in regards to the Direct Relationship between Black and Latinos and the NYS Department of Corrections empowered me to see the bigger picture of my incarceration and understanding that I must pass this empowering information along to others. I am currently the Secretary of an inmate organization called Caribbean African Unity. I utilize this vehicle to continue to educate others about the Direct Relationship between Blacks and Latinos and the NYS Department of Corrections but more so about the Crime Generative Attitudes that must be combated while incarcerated. I am committed to performing my job in jamming the revolving door of recidivism and implementing Non-Traditional Approaches to combat this Direct Relationship that is claiming the lives of so many of our youth as it did mine back in 1986. I would like to conclude my learning experience with a quote from the Green Haven Correction Facilities Political Action Committee, "It is time that state prisoners participate in solving the critical problems that affect their own community."

References
Clines, Francis X., "Ex-Inmates Urge Return to Areas of Crime to Help," The New York Times, December 23, 1992, p. A1

Fisher, Brian. Before Joint Legislative Fiscal Committee, January 27, 2009. Commissioner of the Department of Corrections.

Hinds, Lennox. "Illusion of Justice: Human Rights Violation in the United States," 1978.

Owens, Charles E., "Blacks & Criminal Justice: Looking Back Black" p. 7-14

Toure, Ahat N. N., "The Impact of Criminal Justice on the New York State's African & Latino Population: A Focus on Corrections," June, 1993, p.1

CHAPTER ELEVEN
Try to Understand My Side

Try to understand my side. I was confined decade after decade behind steel bars and concrete bricks and European officers with police sticks. Beginning at the age of seventeen sometimes this shit seems like a big f***ing dream.

Being institutionalized in a corrupt system built on racism and pacifism; Having to adapt to an extremely violent environment or be sliced in my face by individuals who don't understand our flat struggling to capture my identity all along fighting with my inner serenity.

Try to understand my side as I try to explain my pain of being sentenced to life with the criminally insane. Where there is no room to cry because if I sleep on my peers I could die. So I have to clear my eyes and not dwell on my crime; just maintain my focus on doing this time. Shipped up North forty of us on a back of a bus being transported hundreds of miles away from loved ones and family; not having the slightest clue to my overall destiny. The marching orders were to stay strong and watch out for the bootie bandits because they run rampant.

Try to understand my side of being conditioned to fight, stab and extort all those in my circumference on a force pretense of gaining prominence.

What's ironic about this whole situation is that I honored my prison reputation with admiration. Not understand what all this turmoil was doing to my soul. So, I became more rabid and inconsiderate to the feelings of any convict. Sh**, I was from Bed-Stuy, "we got to do or die" and my mother won't be the one wiping her eyes. I was entrenched in the deviant culture where the rules of the game were to be the meanest vulture with a diabolical view of my circumstances. It was far more then taking chances and viewing life with brief glances. I was trapped in ignorance and headed for a return to the essence.

Try to understand my side and what sometimes contribute to my inappropriate tirades. Can you imagine my mother taking the blame for my homicide, so deep that she tried to commit suicide? I still didn't open my eyes. I just acted out more destructive and wrong thinking it was a valuable channel to release frustration and pinned up aggravation. Constantly dealing with racist C.O.s that main objective is to push buttons and get individuals to lose their grip so they can pull out the whip. Struggling to maintain ones dignity while being trapped in a form of purgatory where true friends are absent, God is in a crutch and dealing with suffering is a must. Closed off from humanity and it's a wonder why 90% of us don't lose our sanity.

Try to understand my side. Struggling each day not to just give up and always saying what the f***. Hundreds of men living together in cramped quarter, living by imaginary boarders that sort us and divide us against each other. None of us realizing we are brothers. This environment is bent on mental destruction to break a brother down so he can't function. Sometimes, even I wonder how the hell I survived all these years pinning up my fears, holding back my tears and subduing my cares. Can you really say I am alive or just a dead man walking in a system bent on stalking? My only reprieve is educating myself so I will never have to repeat this morbid defeat. I read and study until my head hurts, my eyes become teary and my mind sometimes get weary. But I keep moving forward because they will never count me amongst the broken men. You see I am determined to WIN!

Try to understand my side and no it's not solely built on pride even though that's what gives me my stride. I denied myself and righteous lady because I knew deep down inside I had to get myself ready. It has become a task for me to really love a woman. Is that really a sin? Living more than half of your life in prison has to be factored in.

So when I love I love deep, deep from within and I push back the many years of conditioning. I do admit I expect a lot from my queen, but it's not about being mean. You see I have a dream like Dr. Martin Luther King. But mine is to gain a righteous wife and bring children to life.

Live together in total happiness for eternity but that's going to take hard work and mutual commitment so excuse me if at times I vent.

Try to understand my side, granted there may be unwarranted outbursts where I holler and curse but that does not erase the love! Yeah, it may hurt, but if the relationship is strong then we should have no problem carrying it on. This is where a good friend like you fitting not to judge right from wrong but give rational input to keep the relationship strong. I sincerely appreciate everything that you are doing for us and please note that my love is not built on lust but TRUST. It really hurt me to hear that you was disturbed by my emotional tirade and by no means is the poem vindication or justification for my wayward actions. It is just a poem to let you know that sometimes I seem all alone. I know it's corny and may seem snide but it's just a little something to get you to understand my side!

CHAPTER TWELVE
A Word to the Youth

I write this letter as I sit in a poorly lit dormitory with fifty-nine other men in a prison with a population of eighteen hundred prisoners. I would like to share a part of myself with you in the hopes that my experience may somehow shed light and benefit someone whose about to go through what I am enduring day by day. First, you should know that living in a cell has been a part of my sad reality for twenty-three years.

First, let me say that I do not ask for any sympathy whatsoever. I can remember an "Old Timer" schooling me at the beginning of my bid (time). "Sympathy is a counterfeit emotion for a sucker and there's no room for suckers in this mean world of ours." In addition, I now have come to recognize the destructive mentality largely responsible for my situation. I am now forty years old and I spent the prime years of my life incarcerated in the New York Department of Correctional Services. The purpose of this letter is to give a backdrop to my life and those factors that lead me to prison at such an early age in my life.

I was raised in Brooklyn, NY, the Bedford-Stuyvesant section, in a notorious housing project called Marcy. My mother worked in Correction on Riker's Island and is now a retired corrections officer. So you can somewhat imagine the type of disciplinarian household I grew up in. My father worked as a laborer in many fields. May he rest in peace. As I grew up the struggle for necessities is something that I was not alienated from. I knew first-hand what it was like not to have. There were many mornings when breakfast was not served in my home and it was not because someone was too lazy to prepare a meal. I also recall waking up several Christmas mornings and not being able to tell it was Christmas. Can you envision a child waking up Christmas morning with joy in his heart, running to the Christmas tree and finding nothing under it? Returning back to bed with tears in his eyes and a cold heart. However, to compensate for a lack of material possessions there was a strong work ethic that nurtured responsibility in my household.

Crime for me started at a young age. It came in the form of stealing penny candies from the neighborhood candy store. Many times children do things for the sheer satisfaction of getting over. I think that best explains my behavior at that young age. I guess I can say I liked the feeling I felt from getting over. It became more of a challenge than a need. Marcy projects is known for having some of the toughest guys in Brooklyn. Growing up with these images right outside my door had a major impact on my mental and behavioral development. In my feeble mind, I felt that I had to live up and emulate these bad guy images in order to be accepted and fit in to my environment. It is a known fact that negative peer pressure for a young man growing up in the inner city can be crushing at times. Especially if there is no viable infrastructure to combat the negative peer pressure that is prevalent in the inner city. I had the warped impression that the amount of respect a man receives from his peers defines him. Therefore, I chose, "Respect from my peers instead of Praise from my parents."

In an effort to obtain this illusion of respect, violence was something I sadly indulged in. In the initial stage, violence came in the form of verbal arguments that would eventually lead to fistfights. In an effort to gain so-called respect from my peers this violence would escalate to using knives and handguns. It was as if I had to project a false image of myself to others. Violence became my mask that I wore proudly at times. It became a very intricate part of me. As I look back, I see myself looking for friendship and acceptance in all the wrong places. I did not look for it in the proper places; like with those positive family members that surrounded me or inside my school in teachers or guidance counselors. I did not even look in my community for that positive leadership or guidance amongst the elders and the nine to fivers because in my illusionary world they were all square and did not truly understand my plight or the hidden pain I had pent-up. Therefore, I looked to the older guys from my hood for that leadership. They saw that I had heart (courage), exploited my ignorance and put a gun in my hand; then I began to demand my respect through the barrel of a gun.

I thought that money was the key to manhood because with money came the acceptance of girls and the acquiring of gold jewelry; the symbols of ghetto success. I labeled it the three "G's"; Girls, Gold and Guns. The abundance of these symbols made me feel secure and worth something in life. They gave my life meaning. During my early adolescent years, having these symbols of ghetto success seemed to encourage me to be more violent and self-destructive because they made my mask tighter and fashionable. It seems like the greater the acceptance of my peers; the more violent I was inclined to be.

So in my pursuit for what I deemed respect, I totally lacked the value of human life or property because I had yet to feel any negative consequence. Everything was going according to plan; a plan that I had no idea of its end. That is what happens when you live day by day with no real focus on life. It is a cold world out there and this coldness is not only limited to disadvantaged communities such as Bed-Stuy. This same coldness is inbreeded in the hearts and minds of our youth. I supplied the only heat I had available and it was the heat of a gun, the heat of peer pressure and in the heat of the moment is what best explains my involvement in causing another person's death. The heat of the moment is a reaction rather than a conscious thought. I, like many other youth are spending decades in prison because we refused to think, we refused to listen and refused to look at life in a long-term perspective. Instead, we chose to go with the moment instead of utilizing simple rational thinking. It is hard thinking outside the box when the box is suffocating you.

Now I sit in the custody of the New York State Department of Corrections and there are times when even I cannot believe I am serving a seventeen and a half years prison sentence. All because I refused to be a thinker and opted to be a follower. Now that I am forty years old, not only do I fully understand the error of my ways, I constantly look to make amends for my past actions. I look back at my fast lived childhood and recount the hurt caused to victims. I also look back at the hurt I have caused my own family.

During my many years of incarceration, I have begun to examine my behavior from a more critical perspective. The key elements that contributed to my incarceration and negative behavior was that I allowed others to identify my reality. By doing this, I allowed the course of my life to be set without questioning or examining other people's motives. That is a key point because when we allow others in our life and we do not examine and critically seek their motives we allow them to have control over our lives. It will be unfair for me not to mention that there are social economic conditions in the Black communities that contributed to negative youth behavior. These are factors that have been proven to breed crime such as racism, miseducation and under-education; unemployment, under employment, family breakdown and drugs. These societal ills are prevalent in areas where there is a large concentration of Black youth. Many reports and documentaries prove that communities infested with these Crime Generative Factors account for the large influx of youth in prison from those communities. It just illustrates that if we are going to create an even playing field for our youth we must analyze things holistically and with a very critical eye.

What I would like to express to the youth who are struggling with street life is that life is short and we must appreciate every breath we take. Life is more than a pair of Jordans, a truck or acceptance from the crowd. In addition, street life is for people who do not want a future because the only future street life is going to lead you to prison or death. There is no in-between either you're going to die in the streets in your pursuit to gain symbols of ghetto success or you're going to fall victim to the criminal justice system and spend decades on lock down. Then you just might die in here. Therefore, it is no win situation when you choose Street Life over LIFE itself. After living more than half my life in prison, I can say that this is no place for any youth to be. There have been many nights when I cried, scared of the reality that this situation may actually be my end. The possibility that I many never make it out of prison is something that I must live with daily.

The achievements of ghetto success may be appealing to those lacking a sense of self and a sense of direction. However, it is an achievement that is not worth spending one's life in a cell or living in a controlled environment where every minute of the day someone watches you or you are told what to do and how to do it. As youth, we must begin to think for ourselves and seek out those positive brothers and sisters in our communities. They are there and ready and willing to assist. Nevertheless, if you do not ask then you do not get assisted.

A man is not defined by respect that is garnished from the barrel of a gun. Seriously, think about it. How can you gain respect through fear? That type of respect does not last long at all because sooner or later fear runs out. Then you do not have respect, you have an enemy who wants revenge. Girls, gold jewelry or any other material possession does not define success. Respect comes with responsibility and reasoning right from wrong. Success is measured by your commitment to your community; to rid it of those social ills that negatively contribute to the incarceration of so many people. If I could ask one thing of those misguided youth, it would be to please listen to me. My heart cries every time I see another young brother come through the door with a life sentence because I know first-hand the pain he will go through. I know what his chances are for others to exploit, severely injure or abuse him. I know the unbearable pain that his family will go through as long as he remains incarcerated.

Many times young incarcerated men do not look at the impact incarceration causes their family. They just look at themselves and the long stretch of time they have to do. They blame everybody in the world except themselves for their current situation; never looking outside themselves and at the people who truly love them. Take my mother for instance she was totally unaware of my lifestyle. While incarcerated my mother took the blame on herself as opposed to acknowledging my role in this behavior. She felt that she went wrong somewhere in raising me. With her youngest son in prison at seventeen years old and not eligible for release for seventeen and a half years, she thought it was her fault. This was just too much for her and she under-went several severe emotional breakdowns and saw her deathbed twice. I thank God for her. Her wisdom and strength have helped me to survive through this ordeal.

My mother's struggle to come to grips with my situation took the veils of violence, street life and negative behavior off my eyes.

We must not wait until we are faced with crippling situations such as mine to recognize the pit falls of our ways of living. We must begin to look at life with a new vigor. A vigor that states a gun can get me perceived peer respect, but a pen can get me a degree. A vigor that states the spirituals are past being enough, that laughter and dance are definitely not enough and that the tears and blood have been way too much that we must realize the time is now. We and only we must help ourselves.

CHAPTER THIRTEEN
Wonder!

Did you ever wonder why the sun rises each day or why the sky is blue? Well, just look at the beauty within you.

If the rise of the sun puzzles you, do not worry the same happens to me, too. So close your eyes and enjoy the sojourn of this internal burn.

Did you ever wonder how in the world did our two paths cross? Well, frankly I am with you; but not off course. I try hard to figure why God has blessed me with a gift such as you. All my life you have danced around my dreams so it seems. Now, I have the pleasure of communicating with you on a very special level.

It is kind of ironic because some say I used to be evil like the devil. Now, I am blessed with a beautiful angel. You are indeed heaven sent and I must bow down to my knees and repent.

Did you ever wonder how my life manifested itself in this way? Spending twenty plus years in an institution of abysmal decay; many years of inner crying, spiritually dying but morally surviving.

A childhood filled with frightening violence; captured by the lure of street life at an age of internal strife. Who is the blame for my teenage carnage? Is it institutional racism, family breakdown, unemployment or how about the infamous mis-education? No excuses; it was my warped decision making and outward abuses. At this time in my life I really need you to understand me for me and not my past history or criminality that most people use to define me.

Did you ever wonder about your life? It's success, emotional turmoil and all those characteristics that create that special you? I sit many nights and feel your touch, savoring your gentle clutch, wishing I could feel your warm embrace and share in your magnificent grace. I envision your smile and its sincerity lightens my heart because I understand you are my intricate part. You are the one that is going to give me my brand new start. One thing you never have to worry about is me walking out. I am your man and the creator upstairs has the master plan.

Did you ever wonder why you are my Kindred Spirit? Do not just feel it, never forget it. Your soul and mine are entwined as one working through the obstacles like a mother with her first born son. Our union is not built on sexual intercourse. This is why we have the ability to reach into each other's minds and feel the force.

Our spirits are like rivets locking us together forever to share in our mental pleasure. We do not have to be in each other's arms to feel this connection. Just knowing that each other is alive is what gives us satisfaction. One day soon we will look into one another eyes and there will be no surprise to the love we hold because God have revealed our souls.

Did you ever really wonder who Richard R. Jackson is? Well let me tell you. He is a man that treasures your existence and can't wait to have you in his presence. He is a man that is built on integrity and appreciates honesty. He loves a woman who can be herself and support her man, regardless of the situation at hand. He has run into some difficulties in his life, however, he is pushing on and staying strong.

He appreciates his life but yearns to have a wife. It is hard for people to understand him because it is hard for him to trust and let people in. He's not like most men because he likes to cuddle and kiss but you will be hard pressed to get him to admit this.

I don't want you ever wondering about Richard R. Jackson; just know in your heart that he is a man of action.

Did you ever wonder why Black men and Black women have so much difficulty establishing and maintain a relationship? It is because living in this dictatorship has caused us to lose respect and obscure the objective.

Never forget the theme of Willie Lynch and its essence. The union of Black male and female has the power to combat all ills. We are the original people and the originators of civilized society. Our genetic make-up is superior, not inferior; but they have placed us under the radar.

From kings and queens who reigned supreme reduced to a people who have nothing but hopes and dreams. Our cultural and moral identity eradicated by overt racism and replaced with egoism, sexism and materialism. Our ultimate potential in history will one day be realized. Let us just pray it is way before our demise.

CHAPTER FOURTEEN
Brothers Killing Brothers

Brother killing Brothers over a color; not really seeing or understanding each other. Not looking into why they originated. What happens to brotherly love overriding oppression and depression?

D*** this sh** is crazy because mothers are burying baby after baby and prisons are being filled up with young men with no vision.

All brothers do is throw up hand signs not realizing they fell into a systematic design aimed at halting the revolution and finding solutions.

Blacks kill Blacks while others sit back and record the stats. Where are the elders that once held the reins to our community; strong enough to step forth and give these brothers and sister direction instead of rejection. Or have the youth produced so much fear that our race just threw their hands in the air and said they don't f***ing care!

How quickly we forget the 60's and 70's. The same youth organizations existed but under different prefixes. Some say back then they stood for something but the bodies dropped, the drugs popped and the violence was non-stop. However, the community took charge and refused to succumb to the hum drum of the propelling deviant culture.

No one says a word when big pharmaceutical pundits market prescription drugs that kill by the hundreds. We protest because Bush went into Iraq but say nothing while OPEC pats each other on the back.

Our brothers and sisters are killing each other over colors and the matrix is on the conscious people because we do not recognize the hurt, pain and abandonment that our young feel. We are just flaring up and looking at them in disgust. Not seeing deep within that all they need is someone to trust. It does not matter, Crip, Blood or Latin King. They are all saying something. Yeah, yeah. They are running aimlessly but they are their only family. We cannot judge if we do not seek to address the root cause. Hold up, pause…think for a minute!

My son, my daughter, we all must come together to regain order. We cannot wait on Condoleezza Rice because she's on Capitol Hill running through a European drill. We can forget about Colin Powell. He is just foul. He forgot what it is to be poor, black and in real trouble. There will not be any legislative action because like Bob Marley said, "Some people have hopes and dreams while others have ways and means."

The White House won't be sending down any directive. Oh, I forgot the Patriot Act I & II. So we cannot keep turning our nose up in disgust at the brothers killing brothers and sisters, too; the wise thing to do it to check you. Remember, when the hand sign was a bald up right fist thrust in the air. The colors were red, black and green. We marched for freedom, fought for equality organized for revolution and mobilized for positive evolution.

Well times have changed and our community has been rearranged. Brothers are killing brothers and we stand by and look at each other instead of building viable infrastructure. There must be a hands-on approach to this deviant culture that has the potential of eroding the core of our existence.

Believe me no one wants to Ride or Die. So let's begin to teach our Brothers and Sisters that they can indeed fly high!

CHAPTER FIFTEEN
Tears Fall from My Heart

Tears Fall from My Heart with wrenching pain that keeps me dizzy; however, I stand strong in the mist of adversity, even though my education never took me to a prestigious university.

I struggle daily to stay alive, feeling comatose at times, assistance is rare in my lonely atmosphere, but I bare the storm even though most of the time I find myself all alone.

You will never understand my pain unless you felt Massa's whip on your back and with each crack of the skin I maintain an inner grin because deep down inside I know in the end I will indeed WIN.

Tears Fall from My Heart every time my brother is brutally beaten by the cops and all my people do is march.

Every time my sisters give up their sacred center for a hit on a pipe or for some gear they think is Tight.

The rich blood of my people is entwined with racism and the systemic design of Amerikkk's poverty.

Everyone is banking on winning the lottery or OTB. That is fixed for us forget the meaning of the crucifix.

Please understand that it is spirituality that will ultimately set us free and it is the poverty that has us crouched down on one knee hoping for a victory.

Tears Fall from My Heart when I witness the devastation of hurricane Katrina and the inadequate response from FEMA.

President George Bush was playing golf and making deals, while thousands of people went five whole days without meals.

Richard Jackson

"Our country tis of thee; sweet land of liberty."

Only rings true if you do not live in poverty, never been convicted of a robbery and can stomach America's Debauchery.

This is not a love poem but an expression of my deep-rooted pain and frustration, from living on plantation after plantation, enduring oppression and not having an outlet for my subjugation.

Tears Fall from My Heart and rolls down my cheeks with a burning fire that ache my soul.

Giving me the gruesome feeling of being totally out of control.
Only to reach my lips and be extinguished by the fluids on my tongue which takes the pain deeper within. So don't ask me why I hardly grin.
Don't get it twisted I am not bitter, emotionally rung or upset; I am just in dire need of a valuable outlet.

Most judge me by my crime and not by my inherited sublime.
Is it a crime to enact an embargo that stunts countries children the ability to grow or how about to steal an inaugural; with the Supreme Courts stamp of approval?

Is it a crime to yearn to be free after admitting to murder in the second degree or is spending twenty plus years of my life in prison really necessary.

I thought we lived in a democratic society based on democracy or is it because I do not embrace mainstream theology and will not bow down to the powers that be?

Tears fall from my heart non-stop but I will remain strong no matter how long the suffering goes on.

The carnage in my life has equipped me to be a strong a man. Do not feel sorry for me or attempt to wipe the tears away from my heart because they are an intricate part of my brand new start.

I need to feel the burn on my cheeks; they are a constant reminder that I am yet to reach my peak.

My present condition has by no means usurped my power, it has given me the uncanny consciousness and strength not to cower and hold my head high and face the coming hour!

I will not be demolished like the New York Twin Towers.

TEARS FALL FROM MY HEART AND I PRAY TO GOD THEY WILL NEVER STOP!!

BIOGRAPHY

Richard R. Jackson served twenty-six years consecutively in various New York State Correctional Facilities. He was released on April 28, 2011. During his incarceration he assisted in initiating and facilitating the Resurrection Study Group (RSG), Alcohol and Substance Abuse Treatment (ASAT), Alternative to Violence Program (AVP) and was very instrumental in bringing the Youth Assistance Program (YAP) to the Greenhaven Correctional facility and changing the model from Scared Straight to Steer Straight.

Mr. Jackson earned a Certificate in Ministry from The New York Theological Seminary, an Associates in Liberal Arts and Social Science from Dutchess Community College and is two classes shy from earning his Bachelors degree in Organizational Management from Nyack College.

Mr. Jackson is currently assistant director of "One Life Two Live"; a community safety program that addresses violence on a direct street level in Schenectady, New York. He is a proud member and re-entry specialist for Community Fathers Inc. Mr. Jackson volunteers weekly to facilitate re-entry classes at Schenectady County Jail. In addition, he speaks at secure Youth facilities in New York State.

He has worked with the Center for Law and Justice in Albany, New York, New Choices Recovery as a substance Abuse counselor and at the Youth Advocate Program as a youth advocate. Mr. Jackson is dedicated and continues to perform community work specifically in the areas of youth development and re-entry.